EXPOSITORY INSIGHTS ON JOHN 13-17

A WORKBOOK FOR EXPOSITORY PREACHING

By David A. Christensen

© 2017 by David A. Christensen

All rights reserved. No part of this book may be reproduced, stored in a retrieval system, or transmitted, in any form or by any means, electronic, mechanical, photocopying, recording or otherwise, except as permitted by US or UK copyright laws, without the prior permission of the author. Requests for information may be addressed to:

> The Rephidim Project
> P.O. Box 145
> Gorham, ME 04038

Scripture quotations not otherwise noted are taken from the NEW AMERICAN STANDARD BIBLE®, Copyright © 1960, 1962, 1963, 1968, 1971, 1972, 1973, 1975, 1977, 1995 by the Lockman Foundation.

All quotations from the Greek text are from:
Nestle, E., Nestle, E., Aland, B., Aland, K., J., Martini, C. M., & Metzger, B. M. (1993). *The Greek New Testament* (27th ed). Stuttgart: Deutsche Bibelgesellschaft.

Cover by Shirley Douglas at Douglas Design, www.sdouglasdesign.com

ISBN-13: 978-0692849545
ISBN-10: 0692849548

The
REPHIDIM
Project

P.O Box 145
Gorham, ME 04038

ACKNOWLEDGEMENTS

I am deeply indebted to Dr. John A. Sproule, Chairman of the New Testament and Greek Department at Grace Theological Seminary from 1976-1986, who instilled in me a love for Greek exegesis during my student days. I had the privilege of not only taking numerous classes from John but of serving as his grading assistant for two years. John welcomed me into his home and invested in my heart. He gave me a copy of *A Greek Grammar of the New Testament and Other Christian Literature* by F. Blass and A. Debrunner when I graduated. Every time I read his inscription in the front of the book I am reminded of His investment in my life. John's passion for God's Word infected my soul with a desire to follow his example of exegetical theology. John graduated into glory in 2014 leaving behind a legacy of students like me who had been touched by his teaching. I will always treasure his input and encouragement which has shaped my ministry.

I also thank Dr. S. Lewis Johnson Jr., who taught a summer course at Grace Theological Seminary on the *Greek Exegesis of the Upper Room Discourse*. It was my joy and privilege to study under his teaching, and the origin of many of my reflections in this volume bear the imprint of his love for the Lord and His Word. He devoted his life to the exposition of the Scriptures and stimulated me to do the same with my life.

OTHER BOOKS BY DAVID CHRISTENSEN

TRANSFORMED BY ADOPTION: The Spiritual Life of a Normal Christian, an exposition of Romans 6:1 - 8:17, The Rephidim Project, 2014.

FRIENDS WITH JESUS: Experiencing the Depths of Spiritual Intimacy, an exposition of John 13-16, The Rephidim Project, 2017.

ABBREVIATIONS OF SOURCES CITED

ATR – Robertson, A. T. *A Grammar of the Greek New Testament in the Light of Historical Research.* Broadman Press, Nashville, Tennessee, 1934.

BAGD – Arndt, William F., and Gingrich, F. Wilbur. *A Greek-English Lexicon of the New Testament and Other Early Christian Literature.* Second Edition Revised and Augmented from Walter Bauer's Fifth Edition, 1958. The University of Chicago Press, 1979.

BD – Blass, F. and Debrunner, A. *A Greek Grammar of the New Testament and Other Early Christian Literature.* A translation and Revision of the ninth-tenth German edition by Robert W. Funk. The University of Chicago Press, 1961.

BERN – Bernard, J.H. *A Critical and Exegetical Commentary on the Gospel According to St. John,* edited by A.H. McNeile. Edinburgh: T. & T. Clark, 1976.

BRO – Brown, Raymond E. *The Gospel of John in The Anchor Bible Commentary,* Doubleday & Company, Inc. 1970.

BUR – Burton, Ernest De Witt. *Syntax of the Moods and Tenses in New Testament Greek,* The University of Chicago Press, 1900. Kregel Publications Edition, 1976. Second Printing, 1978.

CAR – Carson, D.A. *The Farewell Discourse and Final Prayer of Jesus: An Exposition of John 14-17.* Baker Book House Company, 1980.

CAR2 – Carson, D.A. *The Difficult Doctrine of the Love of God.* Crossway Books, 2000.

CHE - Cheney, Johnstone M. *The Life of Christ in Stereo: The Four Gospels Combined as One.* Edited by Stanley A. Ellison, Western Baptist Seminary Press, 1969.

DM – Dana, H. E., and Mantey, Julius R. *A Manual Grammar of the Greek New Testament.* The Macmillan Company, 1927. Reprinted 1957.

ESV – *The Holy Bible: English Standard Version.* Crossway Bibles, A publishing ministry of Good News Publishers, 2001.

GDT – Godet, Frederic Louis. *Commentary on John's Gospel.* Reprint of the 1886 edition by Funk & Wagnalls. Kregel Publications, 1978. Reprinted 1980.

HAN – Hanna, Robert. *A Grammatical Aid to the Greek New Testament.* Baker Book House, 1983. This edition was originally published in 1980 by the Summer Institute of Linguistics in two volumes.

HBM – *The New Testament in Modern English: Centenary Translation*. Translated by Helen Barrett Montgomery, The Judson Press, 1952 by The American Baptist Publication Society. Seventeenth Printing, 1968.

LN – Louw, Johannes, P.; Nida, Eugene A. *Greek-English Dictionary of the New Testament based on Semantic Domains*, (electronic ed., of the 2nd edition). New York: United Bible Societies, 1996.

LS – *A Lexicon Abridged from Liddell and Scott's Greek-English Lexicon*. Oxford: At the Clarendon Press. Printed in Great Britain at the University Press, Oxford, 1871. Reprinted in 1980.

METZ – Metzger, Bruce M. *A Textual Commentary on the Greek New Testament: A Companion Volume to the United Bible Societies' Greek New Testament, Third Edition*. On behalf of and in cooperation with the Editorial Committee of the United Bible Societies' Greek New Testament, Kurt Aland, Matthew Black, Carlo M Martini, Bruce Metzger, and Allen Wikgren. United Bible Societies, 1971. Corrected Edition, 1975.

MEY – Meyer, Heinrich August Wilhelm. *A Critical and Exegetical Hand-Book to the Gospel of John*. Translated from the Fifth Edition of the German by William Urwick and edited by Frederick Crombie, Funk & Wagnalls, Sixth Edition, 1884. Reprinted in 1983.

MHT - Moulton, James Hope; Howard, Wilbert Francis; and Turner, Nigel. *A Grammar of New Testament Greek*. Edinburgh: T. & T. Clark, Third Edition, 1978.

MM – Moulton, James Hope and Milligan, George. *The Vocabulary of the Greek New Testament Illustrated from the Papyri and Other Non-Literary Sources*. Wm. B. Eerdmans Publishing Company. One Volume Edition, 1930. Reprinted, 1976.

MOR – Morris, Leon. *The Gospel According to John: The English Text with Introduction, Exposition, and Notes*. The New International Commentary on the New Testament, F.F. Bruce, General Editor. Wm. B. Eerdmans Publishing Company, 1971.

MOU – Moule, C.F.D. *An Idiom Book of New Testament Greek*. Second Edition. Cambridge University Press, 1959, reprinted, 1979.

NASB – *New American Standard Bible*. Updated Edition by Zondervan Bible Publishers, 1999.

NIDNTT – *The New International Dictionary of New Testament Theology*. Colin Brown, General Editor. Zondervan Publishing House, 1976.

NIV – *The Holy Bible: New International Version*. Zondervan Bible Publishers, 1978.

SLJ – S. Lewis Johnson, Private Notes, from Greek Exegesis of the Upper Room Discourse, Grace Theological Seminary, 1983.

RIEN – Rienecker, Fritz. *A Linguistic Key to the Greek New Testament*. Edited by Cleon Rogers, Jr. Regency Reference Library from Zondervan Publishing House, 1980.

ROB – Robertson, A.T. *A Harmony of the Gospels for Students of the Life of Christ.* Harper & Row, Publishers, 1922.

TDNT – *Theological Dictionary of the New Testament*, edited by Gerhard Kittel. Translator and Editor Geoffrey W. Bromiley. Wm. B. Eerdmans Publishing Company, 1964. Eleventh Printing, 1981.

TG – Thomas, Robert L., and Gundry, Stanley N. *A Harmony of the Gospels with Explanation and Essays*, Moody Press, 1978.

TRE – Trench, Richard Chevenix. *Synonyms of the New Testament.* Wm. B. Eerdmans Publishing Company. Ninth Edition published in London in 1880. Reprinted in 1975.

TABLE OF CONTENTS

LIST OF ABBREVIATIONS	5
STRUCTURAL ANALYSIS	11
JOHN 13	15
JOHN 14	43
JOHN 15	89
JOHN 16	125
JOHN 17	159

STRUCTURAL ANALYSIS

FIRST STEP: SEGMENTING THE LARGER PASSAGE

The first step in expository preaching is to segment the Bible book into sections. Each segment should be a complete unit of thought. Expository preaching is not so much verse by verse preaching as it is unit of thought preaching. Compare the paragraphing of the Nestle-Aland Greek New Testament with several English translations to determine the units of thought based on the decisions of the editors. The goal is to segment the larger passage of Scripture into units of thought. Verse by verse exposition often loses the author's main idea in the details of the text. Effective exposition strives to expose the original author's units of thought so that people can think through the passage as the biblical author intended. Each unit of thought becomes the foundation for the sermon.

SECOND STEP: DIAGRAMMING THE UNITS OF THOUGHT

A structural diagram of a unit of thought traces the arrangement of the passage by following various structural clues. The objective is to see the passage and then trace in visual form the grammatical relationships of the clauses. There are excellent tools out there that diagram sentences for the expositor giving rich grammatical information about the passage. However, the danger of these grammatical diagrams is that the expositor gets lost in the details and cannot see the preaching points. The expositor cannot see the forest for the trees. We can become so immersed in the analysis that we cannot summarize the main points. Therefore, I recommend a block diagram for preaching purposes. A block diagram blocks out the main clauses in a visual format. We want to see what the author was trying to emphasize rather than what we want to emphasize, and we want to preach a sermon not deliver a doctoral dissertation.

A block diagram helps the expositor visualize the structure of the passage just like an electrical schematic helps an electrician visualize the wiring of a device. There are five values of block diagramming.

1) Block diagramming can be used for all genres of literature such as poetry, narrative and prophetic forms of communication in addition to the epistles.

2) Block diagramming is simpler and takes less time than grammatical line diagramming. The busy pastor is more likely to use block diagramming and will find it more useful to gain the information needed for sermon preparation.

3) Block diagramming emphasizes the important information for preaching. Most of the information vital to sermon preparation pertains to the major clause and phrase breakdown. The many exegetical commentaries and tools available can provide the more specific and technical information as needed.

4) Block diagramming is more visual than other forms of structural analysis. The goal is to diagram the entire unit of thought on one page so that the expositor can see the main preaching points. A diagram needs to be visual to be effective. It must summarize the text in a visual way so the expositor can easily see the structure of the passage. The block diagram

helps the expositor summarize the essential issues for sermon preparation quickly and efficiently.

5) Block diagramming leads easily into a sermon outline. A good sermon outline should not go beyond the first (and in some cases second) level of structure. The main preaching points are the skeleton of the sermon. A sermon that becomes more detailed than that risks losing the people because they cannot follow the complexities of detailed outlines. A block diagram visualizes the main preaching points for the expositor.

Developing a block diagram:

Purpose: To visualize the flow of thought – to picture the structure.

Use the following format for your diagram.

Copy and paste the text into a word processing document. Keep the words of the text in order as you go through the next steps. Word order is important for exposition. Use the "enter" and "tab" commands to break the passage down according to major and minor ideas. Major ideas are on the left of the page, and subordinate ideas move progressively to the right. Parallel ideas should begin in the same column as the corresponding idea.

If you are using paper and pencil instead of a computer, you should divide the paper into vertical columns. Write the words of the text in order breaking down the text into major and minor clauses with the major to the left and the minor to the right.

Distinguish between major and minor clauses.

The expositor must distinguish between the major and minor clauses in a unit of thought which is an interpretive process that is basic to structural analysis. Identify the independent clauses first. The main verbs in each sentence are the keys to identifying the independent clauses since independent clauses, containing both a subject and a predicate, can stand alone in a sentence. In the Greek text, main verbs are indicatives, imperatives, and subjunctives that are not introduced by a subordinate particle. Participles, Infinitives and any indicative that is part of a subordinate clause are not main verbs. In the English text, it is sometimes harder since many translations turn subordinate verbs into main verbs for English readers. The translations that follow a dynamic equivalence method of translating are more likely to muddy the distinction between independent and dependent clauses. Therefore, the expositor should use English translations that follow a word for word translating method more closely to avoid the confusion. Comparing multiple translations will also help the expositor determine the main verbs in each sentence.

Enter each clause or phrase on a new line in the diagram. Decide the level of importance for each clause and move it to the right or left in the diagram based on your interpretive decision. Major clauses move to the left and minor clauses to the right. Independent clauses should be to the left in the diagram and dependent clauses to the right. You will often make decisions the first time through the process that you will change later as you look more carefully at the text. Keep working with the interpretive decisions until you arrive at your schematic of the passage.

Conjunctions are the keys that unlock the structure.

> Connectives are the hinges on which the passage swings. The conjunctions form the structural clues in the passage. There are a wide variety of such clues, and they are important to structural analysis out of proportion to their relative size. Each connective should start a new line in the diagram. The following is a sample (not exhaustive) list of connectives.
>
> a) Coordinating (and, nor, for, but, neither/nor, either/or, both/and, not only, but also)
> b) Contrasting (but, except)
> c) Emphatic (truly, certainly, in fact)
> d) Logical (therefore, then, wherefore, so)
> e) Transitional (and, wherefore, so)
> f) Subordinating (when, because, since, although, that, where)
> g) Comparative (as, just as, like)

Other clues help form the block diagram.

> Several other grammatical clues are also useful for block diagramming. The following is a sample of such clues.
>
> a) Participles (generally distinguished in English by the "ing" ending of the word)
> b) Infinitives (generally distinguished in English by the preposition "to")
> c) Repeated words (repetition is an important visual clue)
> d) Change of speaker is an important clue in conversational narrative
> e) Change of subject is an important clue, particularly in narrative.

THIRD STEP: FRAMING THE MAIN POINTS OF EACH SEGMENT

The clauses on the far left in the block diagram are the main thoughts in the passage. There should be two to five important clauses in each unit of thought. The expositor should principlize these ideas as universal truths. These are the principles to be explained in contemporary terms that the listener can apply to his/her life. The main points should follow the structural diagram. These main points form the outline of the exposition. The skill of the expositor is demonstrated in his/her ability to principlize the main points of the unit of thought in language that the contemporary listener can understand and apply. The expositor seeks to exegete the world of his/her listener to find contemporary life parallels and frame the ideas in those terms. It is important that the expositor works to develop the principles and frame the message for himself and his/her audience. Audience analysis is critical for framing the message effectively. Using the outlines from another person short circuits the process of Bible exposition.

JOHN 13

John 13:1-5

    Now before the Feast of the Passover
    Πρὸ δὲ τῆς ἑορτῆς τοῦ πάσχα
Jesus knowing
εἰδὼς ὁ Ἰησοῦς
    that His hour had come
    ὅτι ἦλθεν αὐτοῦ ἡ ὥρα
        that He would pass over
        ἵνα μεταβῇ
            out of this world to the Father,
            ἐκ τοῦ κόσμου τούτου πρὸς τὸν πατέρα,
        having loved the ones belonging to Him in the world
        ἀγαπήσας τοὺς ἰδίους τοὺς ἐν τῷ κόσμῳ
            unto the end He loved them.
            εἰς τέλος ἠγάπησεν αὐτούς.
    And supper taking place,
    2 καὶ δείπνου γινομένου,
        The devil already having placed into the heart
        τοῦ διαβόλου ἤδη βεβληκότος εἰς τὴν καρδίαν
            that Judas Iscariot of Simon should betray Him,
            ἵνα παραδοῖ αὐτὸν Ἰούδας Σίμωνος Ἰσκαριώτου,
Knowing
3 εἰδὼς
    That the Father had given all things to Him into the hands
    ὅτι πάντα ἔδωκεν αὐτῷ ὁ πατὴρ εἰς τὰς χεῖρας
    and that He had come from God
    καὶ ὅτι ἀπὸ θεοῦ ἐξῆλθεν
    and is going back to God,
    καὶ πρὸς τὸν θεὸν ὑπάγει,
He rose up from the supper
4 ἐγείρεται ἐκ τοῦ δείπνου
    And removed the outer clothes
    καὶ τίθησιν τὰ ἱμάτια
        and grabbing a towel
        καὶ λαβὼν λέντιον
He tied it around himself
διέζωσεν ἑαυτόν·
    Then He poured water into a wash basin
    5 εἶτα βάλλει ὕδωρ εἰς τὸν νιπτῆρα
        And began to wash the feet of the disciples
        καὶ ἤρξατο νίπτειν τοὺς πόδας τῶν μαθητῶν
        and wiped them with the towel which was wrapped around.
        καὶ ἐκμάσσειν τῷ λεντίῳ ᾧ ἦν διεζωσμένος.

PREACHING POINTS

The main verbs all come at the end of the narrative. The central idea of the section would focus on these action verbs. A principle summarizing the actions as a whole would be the main preaching point of the section. The repeated participle (εἰδὼς) would express the two reasons for the principle so there would be two supporting preaching points in the message. The repetition of the participle is the striking structural feature of this section.

Central Idea: (vs. 4-5)

1. (vs. 1-2)

2. (v.3)

Briefly, identify two contemporary life parallels to these verses.

CLP #1

CLP #2

MISSIONAL KNOWLEDGE AND FOOTWASHING

Doing comes from knowing. Action springs from knowledge. Understanding His commission drives His mission. Jesus did not merely perform a spontaneous act of love when He washed the disciples' feet that night. The footwashing was grounded in the knowledge of His mission and intended to teach us about His mission. The symbolic act of washing their feet taught a vital spiritual lesson about His sacrificial mission.

The word translated "knowing" (εἰδὼς) is used twice in this introductory section to the upper room discourse. Both times John uses the perfect active participle to express the knowledge of Jesus. Jesus has known His mission all along. This night is not a surprise to Him. The knowledge is not abstract but concrete and directly tied to His mission (John 7:28-29; 8:14). Jesus knows the Father and carries out the Father's will (John 8:54-55). His knowledge has continuing results for all He is doing on this night (TDNT, 5:118). He knows that "His hour has come" (ἦλθεν αὐτοῦ ἡ ὥρα) to pass over (μεταβῇ) to His Father. His knowledge drives His actions as He teaches us His truth.

The participles should not be translated "although He knew" (concessive use) as if Jesus washed their feet in spite of His knowledge. The participles are best translated "because He knew" (causal use) indicating that Jesus washed their feet because He knew His mission (MEY, 3:386). His knowledge of His mission drove Him to display a final expression of His love for them. What He knows frames the reason for what He did. Why did Jesus wash their feet? He washed their feet because He knew He would die for them. The footwashing and the cross work are connected by the knowledge of His mission.

Jesus knew that the Father "had given all things into His hands" (πάντα ἔδωκεν αὐτῷ ὁ πατὴρ εἰς τὰς χεῖρας). Jesus was sovereign. He knew the unfolding events were in His hands. He had control over whatever would happen. His sovereign knowledge drove His submission to the mission. He chose to die. He could have avoided the death if He had wanted to avoid the death, but He chose to carry out the mission that He had known from eternity past (BERN, 2:456). For the same reason, Jesus chose to wash their feet. The footwashing is a symbolic expression of that same sacrificial love we see in the cross and is grounded in His knowledge of the mission formed in eternity past.

Jesus will teach them through His washing of their feet that His actions have a double meaning. There is a two-fold aspect to what He is doing. He talks about washing and bathing (John 13:8-10) in spiritual terms. The physical foot washing symbolizes a deeper spiritual meaning that they will not understand until later. The footwashing becomes a kind of acted out parable which complements the Lord's Supper being instituted that same evening (SLJ). Footwashing is a holy pantomime – a silent lecture – regarding sacrificial love which we should emulate in our lives too.

Oh, Lord, help me to choose daily a life of sacrificial love for others in the spirit of your love for me! Help me suppress my own selfish desires to wash the feet of those you love with an infinite love.

LOVED IN FULL

John begins his description of the final Passover Supper with the words *"having loved His own who were in the world, He loved them to the end"* (John 13:1). The word order of the Greek text is actually *"to the end He loved them"* placing emphasis on the adverbial phrase *"to the end."* What does John mean by that editorial comment? Is he simply saying that Jesus loved them until the end of His life? This seems rather obvious from the passage and hardly worth emphasizing, as John takes pains to do by placing the phrase ahead of the verb. There is another way to look at the phrase, and it powerfully moves our minds into the mystery of His love. The preposition, "to" (εἰς), indicates purpose (MHT, 3:266). Jesus loved them with the purpose of loving them to the end – the end of His love! The noun translated "end" (τέλος), can also mean complete or full so the phrase can be summarized as completely or fully. He loved them in full. He loved them with the intention of loving them to the fullness of His love so "he gave them the perfect love token" (BD, p.112). John's editorial comment introduces the foot washing that immediately follows this passage. The footwashing was Jesus' love token, showing that He purposely loved them in full – to the fullness of His love. What does it mean when an infinite God, with an infinite capacity to love, intentionally loves us to the fullness of His love? No matter how great the marriage, a husband and wife do not love in full. There is always some element of selfishness in our love. Human love always falls some centimeters short of full love – but not Jesus. He loves us to the fullness of His infinite love. There is not a smidgen of love left unloved – for them – for me – for you! Mind boggling!

John 13:6-11

    So he came to Simon Peter
6 ἔρχεται οὖν πρὸς Σίμωνα Πέτρον·
        And he said to him
        λέγει αὐτῷ·
            Lord, are you going to wash my feet?
            Κύριε, σύ μου νίπτεις τοὺς πόδας;
Jesus answered and said to him
7 ἀπεκρίθη Ἰησοῦς καὶ εἶπεν αὐτῷ·
    What I am doing you do not understand now,
    ὃ ἐγὼ ποιῶ σὺ οὐκ οἶδας ἄρτι,
        but you will comprehend after these things.
        γνώσῃ δὲ μετὰ ταῦτα.

    Peter said to him,
8 λέγει αὐτῷ Πέτρος·
        No, by no means may you wash my feet forever.
        οὐ μὴ νίψῃς μου τοὺς πόδας εἰς τὸν αἰῶνα.
Jesus answered him
ἀπεκρίθη Ἰησοῦς αὐτῷ·
    If I may not wash you, you have no part with me.
    Ἐὰν μὴ νίψω σε, οὐκ ἔχεις μέρος μετ' ἐμοῦ.

    Simon Peter said to him,
9 λέγει αὐτῷ Σίμων Πέτρος·
        Lord, not my feet only but also the hands and the head.
        Κύριε, μὴ τοὺς πόδας μου μόνον ἀλλὰ καὶ τὰς χεῖρας καὶ τὴν κεφαλήν.
Jesus said to him,
10 λέγει αὐτῷ ὁ Ἰησοῦς·
    The one who has been bathed has no need
    ὁ λελουμένος οὐκ ἔχει χρείαν
        except to wash the feet,
        εἰ μὴ τοὺς πόδας νίψασθαι,
        but he is wholly pure
        ἀλλ' ἔστιν καθαρὸς ὅλος·
    and you are pure,
    καὶ ὑμεῖς καθαροί ἐστε,
        but not all.
        ἀλλ' οὐχὶ πάντες.
            For he had known the one who was betraying him
            11 ᾔδει γὰρ τὸν παραδιδόντα αὐτόν·
            For this reason, he said you are not all pure.
            διὰ τοῦτο εἶπεν ὅτι οὐχὶ πάντες καθαροί ἐστε.

JOHN 13

PREACHING POINTS

The narrative is structured around Peter's expressions followed by Jesus' responses. The preaching points focus on Jesus' responses not Peter's opinions, so the responses of Jesus are placed to the left following each expression of Peter. A blank line is placed between each exchange to highlight the fact that Peter's opinion starts a new segment in the narrative and should be taken with what follows not what precedes. There would be three preaching points in the sermon corresponding to the three responses by Jesus.

Central Idea:

1. (vs.6-7)

2. (v.8)

3. (vs.9-11)

Briefly, identify two contemporary life parallels to these verses.

CLP #1

CLP #2

WHAT?! NOT ME!

Jesus begins to wash the feet of the disciples, and he arrives at Peter in John 13:6. Some think that he starts with Peter, but I think he ends with Peter. This would mean that even Judas had accepted the Lord's washing of his feet - but not Peter. Peter's angst rises inside him with each passing disciple until it explodes when Jesus arrives at him. Curling his feet up under him, he says, *"Lord, do you wash my feet?"* The words sound bland because we do not have any facial expression or verbal intonation to tell us much about Peter's response. However, we do have some clues in the Greek text to help us. The pronouns "you" (σύ) and "my" (μου) are both emphatic in the sentence. Greek uses word order to emphasize certain words, but "my" (μου) is particularly stressed because of its position before the verb. It is clear that Peter's primary concern is himself here. "My feet" shows his pride. Perhaps his voice even dripped with disdain for all the other feet Jesus had washed before him. Peter thinks the other disciples have failed in accepting the foot washing by Jesus.

The verb "wash" (νίπτεις) is a conative present which indicates an attempted action. So the best translation would be *"Lord, are you trying to wash MY feet?"* (MHT, 3:63). Peter's tone of voice would have been incredulous and offended. Peter is incredulous on two counts - that he should need his feet washed and that the Lord should be the one to do it. This is pride masquerading as humility. We, too, can sound so humble in exalting Jesus with our words when we actually are too proud to accept his washing work in our lives. A few verses later, Jesus will highlight this truth by saying, "He who has bathed needs only to wash his feet" (13:10). He uses the same Greek word for wash but in a different form (νίψασθαι). Here it is in the middle voice and indicates permission in this verse. We could translate it, *"He who has bathed needs only to let (allow) his feet to be washed."* We exalt Jesus the most when we allow Him to wash our dirty feet. Jesus is most exalted when we welcome His cleansing.

WITH JESUS OR FOR JESUS?

I like Peter because I am so like Peter. As I meditate on John 13, I see a man who thinks he knows it all when he knows nothing at all. Peter protests the washing of his feet even though Jesus tells him he doesn't understand. Peter replies (13:8) with a passionate *"Never may you wash my feet forever"* (εἰς τὸν αἰῶνα). It is a "forever" denial driven by an ignorant zeal. Jesus gently corrects him, *"If I do not wash you, you have no part with me"* (13:8).

The "me" (ἐμοῦ) is emphatic, and the "with me" (μετ' ἐμοῦ) indicates Jesus is talking about communion, not union. Jesus does not say, *"You have no part in (ἐν) me."* which would have suggested salvation. He says, *"you have no part with (μετ' ἐμοῦ) me."* Jesus is talking about the intimacy of true friendship. A follower of Jesus can miss out on closeness with Jesus through the pride of ignorant passion.

To have a part with Jesus is to share in His ministry. It is "to be his partner, to share in his work" (BERN, 2:461). To have a part with Jesus is also to share a friendship with Him. The word is used in the story of Mary and Martha (Luke 10:42) when Jesus tells Martha, *"Mary has chosen the good part, which shall not be taken away from her."* The good part is the intimacy of true friendship with Jesus that only comes by letting Jesus serve us - letting Jesus wash our feet. Our service for Jesus can become a substitute for intimacy with Jesus.

I like Peter because he catches the point even while missing the truth. Peter immediately asks Jesus to wash not just his feet but also his hands and his head (13:9). He is filled with passionate loyalty, but he still won't let Jesus do as He pleases. It is possible to be very devoted to the Lord yet very wrong at the same time. I, too, feel that temptation to substitute ministry for intimacy and miss the depths of love Jesus longs to share with me.

DIRTY FEET

John 13:10 is an important verse for our spiritual lives. Jesus used a physical action to illustrate a spiritual truth. There are 3 Greek words that bring out the spiritual truth behind the foot washing.

The first word is "the one who has been bathed" (ὁ λελουμένος). This word referred to the washing of the whole body (Heb. 10:22; Acts 9:37). It was used in the literature of the day for bathing the body in the bathing room. An interesting use of the word is found in 2 Peter 2:22 which is best translated *"the sow that washes itself by wallowing in the mire"* (MM, p.381). Some people bathe themselves in the muck of sin, but we have been bathed in the pure water of Jesus. The form of the verb refers to an action that occurred in the past with ongoing results in the present.

The second word is "to wash" (νίψασθαι). This word refers to washing a part of the body like hands or feet (LS, cf. Mark 7:3; Mt. 6:17). The verb is an Aorist Middle Infinitive which is probably best understood as a permissive middle - "to let his feet be washed" (SLJ). This washing is not a washing done to us in the past but a washing we must allow whenever we get spiritually dirty in the present.

The third word is "clean" (καθαρὸς). It is used in tandem with "wholly or completely" (ὅλος). It meant to be pure, innocent or free from offense (LS). The one who has been bathed by Jesus (saved) is wholly pure. Jesus continues by saying "You are pure ones, but not all." Obviously, He is referring to Judas as the exception to purity in their midst even though Jesus has probably washed his feet physically. All who have been spiritually bathed by Jesus (regeneration) are pure on an ongoing basis (present tense) even though they get dirty in life.

The illustration refers to a person who bathes at home but gets dust on his feet walking to the banquet. Such a person only needs to wash his feet to enjoy the banquet. We get dirty as we walk through life and we need to let Jesus wash our feet spiritually to enjoy the intimacy of dinner with Him.

John 13:12-20

Therefore, when he had washed their feet
12 Ὅτε οὖν ἔνιψεν τοὺς πόδας αὐτῶν
And put on his clothes
[καὶ] ἔλαβεν τὰ ἱμάτια αὐτοῦ
And reclined again,
καὶ ἀνέπεσεν πάλιν,
He said to them, do you know what I have done for you?
εἶπεν αὐτοῖς· γινώσκετε τί πεποίηκα ὑμῖν;
You call me the teacher and the master,
13 ὑμεῖς φωνεῖτέ με· ὁ διδάσκαλος, καί· ὁ κύριος,
And you speak well, for I am.
καὶ καλῶς λέγετε· εἰμὶ γάρ.
If therefore I myself washed your feet
14 εἰ οὖν ἐγὼ ἔνιψα ὑμῶν τοὺς πόδας
The master and the teacher
ὁ κύριος καὶ ὁ διδάσκαλος,
You also ought to wash the feet of one another
καὶ ὑμεῖς ὀφείλετε ἀλλήλων νίπτειν τοὺς πόδας·
For a model, I gave to you
15 ὑπόδειγμα γὰρ ἔδωκα ὑμῖν
That just as I myself have done for you
ἵνα καθὼς ἐγὼ ἐποίησα ὑμῖν
you also do.
καὶ ὑμεῖς ποιῆτε.
Truly, truly I say to you,
16 ἀμὴν ἀμὴν λέγω ὑμῖν,
The servant is not greater than his master
οὐκ ἔστιν δοῦλος μείζων τοῦ κυρίου αὐτοῦ
neither the sent one greater than the one who sent him.
οὐδὲ ἀπόστολος μείζων τοῦ πέμψαντος αὐτόν.
If you know these things,
17 εἰ ταῦτα οἴδατε,
Happy are you if you do these things.
μακάριοί ἐστε ἐὰν ποιῆτε αὐτά.
I am not speaking concerning all of you
18 Οὐ περὶ πάντων ὑμῶν λέγω·
I myself know whom I have chosen
ἐγὼ οἶδα τίνας ἐξελεξάμην·
but in order that the Scripture might be fulfilled
ἀλλ' ἵνα ἡ γραφὴ πληρωθῇ·
The one who eats my bread has raised his heel against me.
Ὁ τρώγων μου τὸν ἄρτον ἐπῆρεν ἐπ' ἐμὲ τὴν πτέρναν αὐτοῦ.
From now on I say to you before it comes to be,
19 ἀπ' ἄρτι λέγω ὑμῖν πρὸ τοῦ γενέσθαι,

In order that you might believe when it comes to be
ἵνα πιστεύσητε ὅταν γένηται
   that I am.
   ὅτι ἐγώ εἰμι.
Truly, truly I say to you,
20 ἀμὴν ἀμὴν λέγω ὑμῖν,
   The one who accepts anyone I might send
   ὁ λαμβάνων ἄν τινα πέμψω
      accepts me,
      ἐμὲ λαμβάνει,
   and the one who accepts me
   ὁ δὲ ἐμὲ λαμβάνων
      accepts the one who sent me.
      λαμβάνει τὸν πέμψαντά με.

PREACHING POINTS

There are four main preaching points in this section. The first preaching point revolves around the question that Jesus asks and answers. The twice repeated expression, "Truly, truly I say to you (ἀμὴν ἀμὴν λέγω ὑμῖν) indicates two parallel preaching points. A parenthetical explanation occurs between these two preaching points. The content change in verse 18 requires a separate preaching point. The central idea should summarize these four points.

Central Idea:

1. (vs.12-15)

2. (vs.16-17)

3. (vs.18-19)

4. (v.20)

Briefly, identify two contemporary life parallels to these verses.

CLP #1

CLP #2

DOING OR KNOWING: WHICH IS MORE IMPORTANT?

The blessing of God is enjoyed by the doing not the knowing, but we must know in order to do God's work. The knowing is necessary for the doing, but the doing is necessary for the blessing. I am struck anew by this truth as I meditate on John 13:17. Jesus has just finished washing the feet of the disciples giving them an example to follow. Jesus says, *"If you know these things, you are blessed if you do them."*

The verse contains a double condition necessary to enjoy God's blessing, but the two conditions are not equal in force. The first condition ("if you know") is a first class condition (εἰ ταῦτα οἴδατε) which assumes that the knowing is a fact - a reality. The first class condition emphasizes the reality of the statement so it could be translated "inasmuch as you know these things" (BD, p.189). The second condition ("if you do these things") is a third class condition (ἐὰν ποιῆτε) which assumes that the doing is uncertain or questionable. Jesus assumes that they know what He has been teaching them, but the doing of it is doubtful (ATR, p.1019).

Both knowing and doing are necessary for blessing, but the doing is less certain than the knowing and, therefore, more critical to the blessing. Jesus cuts to the heart of my spiritual life when He makes this statement. I want to enjoy God's blessing, but I try to achieve that blessing through knowing what to do instead of doing what I know. The struggle in my Christian life is not knowing what to do but doing what I know to do. I can waste a lot of time trying to figure out what to know instead of doing what I already know. If I would do what I already know, I would enjoy His blessing while learning more of what I need to know so I can do more of what He wants me to do.

FOOWASHING: WHAT DOES IT MEAN?

There are at least nine interpretations for the meaning of Jesus' words in John 13:14, *"If I then, the Lord and the Teacher, washed your feet, you also ought to wash one another's feet."* 1) Footwashing is a literal and mandatory ordinance for the church to practice. 2) Footwashing illustrates a spiritual attitude of humble service. 3) Footwashing should be performed as preparation for preaching the gospel. 4) Footwashing is a parable of purification for the disciples. 5) Footwashing is symbolic of the humble union of love within the church. 6) Footwashing is symbolic of the death of Christ. 7) Footwashing is a symbol of baptism. 8) Footwashing is a symbol of the Eucharist. 9) Footwashing teaches the need for penance to cleanse one's sins after baptism (BRO, 2:558-559).

The practice of footwashing as an ordinance is a beautiful and moving expression of love for one another, but I do not think it expresses the teaching of Jesus in this passage. If the washing of the feet is to be understood literally then the bathing of the body must be understood literally as well (v.10). Jesus clearly viewed the bathing as figurative, so the washing of the feet must be figurative as well. If we take the footwashing as mandatory, then we have a problem with Jesus' words in verse 8. *"If I do not wash you (your feet), you have no part with Me."* Many Christians do not practice footwashing as an ordinance which means that they have no part with Christ!

Footwashing is a poignant illustration of a spiritual attitude which should permeate the lives of all who follow Jesus. He served us in humble love so we should serve one another in humble love. The word translated "example" (ὑπόδειγμα, v.15) means a model or pattern intended to stimulate us to emulate

Him (BAGD, p.844). The word translated "ought" (ὀφείλετε, v.14) means that we are obliged to do something. An ought is not a must. Ought is a lesser form of obligation than command. The word meant to owe a debt to someone (TDNT, 5:559). It is the word Paul uses for the obligation for wearing a headcovering by women and not by men (1 Cor. 11:7,10), an obligation few make mandatory, and most view as illustrative. Paul tells us we ought to bear the weaknesses of weaker Christians (Rom. 15:1), and the financial contribution the Gentile believers collected for the saints in Jerusalem was a debt they owed to them – an ought not a must (Rom. 15:27). We ought to express thanks constantly (2 Thess. 1:3; 2:13). Husbands ought to love their wives as their own bodies (Eph. 5:28) and we all ought to love one another (1 John 4:11) including the obligation to lay down our lives for each other (1 John 3:16). We ought to offer hospitality to other believers (3 John 8). These practices are "oughts" not "musts." They are obligatory, not voluntary for all Christians, but they are not ordinances for the church equivalent to baptism and communion.

Peter may have had this experience in mind when he wrote 1 Peter 5:5 (SLJ). "Clothe yourselves with humility toward one another." The verb translated "clothe yourselves" (ἐγκομβώσασθε) is an imperative in the middle voice indicating action done to or for ourselves. The verb (ἐγκομβόομαι) is built on a root word (κόμβος) which means "band" or "knot" and expresses the idea of wrapping a piece of clothing around a naked body tied with band or knot (TDNT, 2:339). The word was used for the action of a slave tying on an apron to serve the master (RIEN, p.765). We have an obligation – an ought – to dress ourselves with a spirit that shows humility before others.

John 13:21-30

After saying these things, Jesus was stirred up in the spirit
21 Ταῦτα εἰπὼν [ὁ] Ἰησοῦς ἐταράχθη τῷ πνεύματι
    And witnessed and said
    καὶ ἐμαρτύρησεν καὶ εἶπεν·
Truly, truly I say to you
ἀμὴν ἀμὴν λέγω ὑμῖν
    that one out of you shall hand me over.
    ὅτι εἷς ἐξ ὑμῶν παραδώσει με.
        The disciples were looking to one another
    22 ἔβλεπον εἰς ἀλλήλους οἱ μαθηταὶ
            being confused about whom he spoke.
        ἀπορούμενοι περὶ τίνος λέγει.
One of his disciples was dining in the place of honor on the chest of Jesus,
23 ἦν ἀνακείμενος εἷς ἐκ τῶν μαθητῶν αὐτοῦ ἐν τῷ κόλπῳ τοῦ Ἰησοῦ,
    whom Jesus loved.
    ὃν ἠγάπα ὁ Ἰησοῦς.
So Simon Peter motioned to this one
24 νεύει οὖν τούτῳ Σίμων Πέτρος
    to ask whoever was he speaking concerning whom
    πυθέσθαι τίς ἂν εἴη περὶ οὗ λέγει.
So leaning back in this way on the chest of Jesus that one said to him
25 ἀναπεσὼν οὖν ἐκεῖνος οὕτως ἐπὶ τὸ στῆθος τοῦ Ἰησοῦ λέγει αὐτῷ·
    Lord, who is it?
    Κύριε, τίς ἐστιν;
Jesus answered
26 ἀποκρίνεται [ὁ] Ἰησοῦς·
    That one is the one to whom I will dip the bit of bread, and I will give to him.
    ἐκεῖνός ἐστιν ᾧ ἐγὼ βάψω τὸ ψωμίον καὶ δώσω αὐτῷ.
        So dipping the bit of bread [and taking] he gave to Judas Simon Iscariot.
        βάψας οὖν τὸ ψωμίον [λαμβάνει καὶ] δίδωσιν Ἰούδᾳ Σίμωνος Ἰσκαριώτου.
        And after the bit of bread at that time, Satan entered into that one.
    27 καὶ μετὰ τὸ ψωμίον τότε εἰσῆλθεν εἰς ἐκεῖνον ὁ σατανᾶς.
        So Jesus said to him, what you do, do quickly.
    λέγει οὖν αὐτῷ ὁ Ἰησοῦς· ὃ ποιεῖς ποίησον τάχιον.
            Now this no one knew of those reclining
        28 τοῦτο [δὲ] οὐδεὶς ἔγνω τῶν ἀνακειμένων
            For what purpose he said to him
        πρὸς τί εἶπεν αὐτῷ·
        for some were thinking,
    29 τινὲς γὰρ ἐδόκουν,
            Because Judas had the money box
        ἐπεὶ τὸ γλωσσόκομον εἶχεν Ἰούδας,
        that Jesus said to him
    ὅτι λέγει αὐτῷ [ὁ] Ἰησοῦς·

JOHN 13

buy whatever we have need for the feast,
ἀγόρασον ὧν χρείαν ἔχομεν εἰς τὴν ἑορτήν,
or for the poor that he should give something.
ἢ τοῖς πτωχοῖς ἵνα τι δῷ.
So taking the bit of bread that one went out immediately.
30 λαβὼν οὖν τὸ ψωμίον ἐκεῖνος ἐξῆλθεν εὐθύς.
And it was night.
ἦν δὲ νύξ.

PREACHING POINTS

The best way to diagram conversational narrative is to identify the key statements in the passage. Jesus makes two key statements in this passage. These two statements form the basis for the two main preaching points. A response from the disciples follows each preaching point so the responses should explain the preaching point. The central idea of the exposition would summarize the overall thought of the passage.

Central Idea:

1. (vs.21-25)

2. (vs.26-30)

Briefly, identify two contemporary life parallels to these verses.

CLP #1

CLP #2

THE ABSALOM SYNDROME

Have you ever been hurt by someone you trusted? Jesus knows your pain. He was "troubled" (ἐταράχθη) in spirit (John 13:21). The same verb was used of Jesus at the death of his friend Lazarus (John 11:33). The word means to be disturbed or stirred up. The noun form was used of riots or revolts in the Roman Empire during the first century (MM, p.625). Jesus' emotions were rioting within Him. There was chaos in His spirit - turmoil in His soul. He was being ripped apart from within because He knew what was coming.

The verb is passive telling us His inner riot was caused by an outside person, namely Judas. Jesus has just quoted from Psalm 41:9 which is a psalm by David after he was betrayed by his son, Absalom, and his trusted adviser, Ahithophel (2 Samuel 15). The parallels are striking. David prefigured Jesus. Absalom and Ahithophel both ate meals with David as loved and trusted confidants in his inner circle. Ahithophel hanged himself after his betrayal (2 Samuel 17:23) just like Judas would soon do. They were friends who ate bread together but lifted up the heel to kick the one who fed them. Like the kick of a mule in the gut, Jesus felt the pain of betrayal.

The closest friends cause the greatest hurts. Betrayal by a loved one is like a kick in the solar plexus. Judas, like Absalom and Ahithophel, was a trusted friend and leader. No one, in the whole company of disciples, suspected he was a traitor. He was honored and trusted to keep the money and was seated in the position of honor at the banquet beside Jesus Himself. Absalom was hugely popular with the people. Ahithophel was respected as a counselor. Respected church leaders sting the most when they betray others in the church. The betrayal of a spouse wounds very deeply. Close friends can turn against us when we least expect it. Jesus knows exactly how you feel for He has felt that inner riot of emotions too. Bring your hurts to the one who has experienced those same hurts and can heal your deepest wounds.

THE SINNER'S CHOICE AND THE SAVIOR'S GRACE

A free choice is not free in the sense of un-influenced. A person chooses to sin based on internal and external influences, but the choice is still a genuine choice.

Judas chose to betray Jesus. He took the piece of bread and *"went out immediately; and it was night"* (John 13:30). John, who loves to contrast light and dark, presents the night as a spiritual, not just physical, darkness. Judas chose to leave the light and join the night. How deep is the darkness that envelopes the soul of the one who chooses to leave the light?!

Satan influenced the choice of Judas *"having already put into the heart of Judas ... to betray Him"* (Jn. 13:2). Jesus dipped the bread and gave it to Judas who ate it and *"Satan then entered into him"* (Jn. 13:27). Jesus commanded Judas, *"What you do, do quickly"* (Jn.13:27). Although possessed by Satan, Judas obeyed Jesus. He carried out the will of the Savior thereby accomplishing the grace of God. The idea originated with Satan, but the command came from Jesus, yet Judas made the choice.

The verb, *"he went out,"* (ἐξῆλθεν) is in the active voice meaning that Judas performed the action. The choice is his choice. The choice is not made for him by either Jesus or Satan. We can only speculate on the internal influences leading to his choice, but he makes the choice. Judas excommunicates himself not just from Jesus but from the disciples. Peter also betrays Jesus on that night, but he chooses to remain connected and so will receive the grace that Judas rejects. Excommunication is the choice of the unrepentant sinner to remove himself from the grace of God.

Judas chose to enter the darkness under the influence of Satan even as he obeyed Jesus. This alchemy of wills led to the death of Christ, planned before the world began, and our salvation, initiated by the grace of God.

John 13:31-35

When therefore he went out,
31 Ὅτε οὖν ἐξῆλθεν,
Jesus said,
λέγει Ἰησοῦς·
    now the Son of Man is glorified
    νῦν ἐδοξάσθη ὁ υἱὸς τοῦ ἀνθρώπου
    and God is glorified in him,
    καὶ ὁ θεὸς ἐδοξάσθη ἐν αὐτῷ·
        [If God is glorified in him],
    32 [εἰ ὁ θεὸς ἐδοξάσθη ἐν αὐτῷ],
        God will also glorify him in himself,
        καὶ ὁ θεὸς δοξάσει αὐτὸν ἐν αὐτῷ,
        and He will glorify him immediately.
        καὶ εὐθὺς δοξάσει αὐτόν.
Little children,
33 τεκνία,
    Still a little while I am with you,
    ἔτι μικρὸν μεθ' ὑμῶν εἰμι·
    You will seek me,
    ζητήσετέ με,
        and just as I said to the Jews
        καὶ καθὼς εἶπον τοῖς Ἰουδαίοις
        that where I, myself, am going
        ὅτι ὅπου ἐγὼ ὑπάγω
        you, yourselves, are not able to come,
        ὑμεῖς οὐ δύνασθε ἐλθεῖν,
    I also say to you now.
    καὶ ὑμῖν λέγω ἄρτι.
A fresh command I am giving to you,
34 Ἐντολὴν καινὴν δίδωμι ὑμῖν,
    That you love one another,
    ἵνα ἀγαπᾶτε ἀλλήλους,
        just as I have loved you
        καθὼς ἠγάπησα ὑμᾶς
    that you, yourselves, also love one another.
    ἵνα καὶ ὑμεῖς ἀγαπᾶτε ἀλλήλους.
By this all shall perceive
35 ἐν τούτῳ γνώσονται πάντες
    That you are disciples to me,
    ὅτι ἐμοὶ μαθηταί ἐστε,
        if you have love among one another.
        ἐὰν ἀγάπην ἔχητε ἐν ἀλλήλοις.

JOHN 13

PREACHING POINTS

The diagram pictures three preaching points, the glory of the cross, the limitations we face in following Jesus on earth and the love we must have for one another. The expositor should summarize the passage with a central idea that combines these three preaching points into one theme.

Central Idea:

1. (vs.31-32)

2. (v.33)

3. (vs.34-35)

Briefly, identify two contemporary life parallels to these verses.

CLP #1

CLP #2

THE GLORY OF THE CROSS

The traitor has left the room to do his evil work. As soon as Judas departed, Jesus said, *"Now is the Son of Man glorified, and God is glorified in Him"* (John 13:31). Right now?! Really? The verb is not a present tense verb although often translated as a present tense. The verb is in the aorist tense which often would be translated *"was glorified"* (ἐδοξάσθη) reinforced by another aorist *"God was glorified in Him."*

Here we see one of the oldest uses of the aorist tense to describe something that has just happened (MHT, 1:135). It has happened so recently that in English we express it best in present time. It is called a "Dramatic Aorist" - an idiom used to express a state or reality which has just been entered (DM, p.198). What event plunged Jesus into this glorified state or reality? Judas left the room. The cross work was now under way. Verse 31 is explained by verse 32 which uses a future tense to describe the same glorified state. *"God will glorify Him immediately"* (δοξάσει) (ATR, p.847).

The cross work of Jesus is His glorification - His finest hour. Glorification refers to the act of displaying the greatness of a person. The greatness of Jesus was most displayed in the cross work of Jesus which began the moment Judas left the upper room. John uses *"glorify"* to refer to the cross (John 12:16, 23). The greatness of the Son is displayed on the cross even as the Son displays the Father's greatness on the cross (John 17:1).

Therefore, whenever we diminish the cross, we diminish Christ. Whenever we devalue the cross, we devalue our Lord. Whenever we ignore the cross, we ignore our Savior. We diminish the cross by exalting human abilities. We devalue the cross by over valuing our methods and skills. We ignore the cross when we promote our solutions to life's problems. Sadly, this describes much of modern, western Christianity. We pull Him down when we puff ourselves up. The result is a popular church that thrives on cheap grace and the latest techniques instead of glorying in the cross of Christ.

THE NEW COMMANDMENT

In what sense is Jesus' command to love one another a new commandment? (John 13:34) God had commanded the Israelites to love both fellow Israelites and strangers in the Mosaic Law (Lev. 19:18,34). *"You shall love your neighbor as yourself."* Jesus had repeated this command (Mark 12:31). Jesus, ratifying the Mosaic Law, commanded us to love God and love our neighbors as the two greatest commandments of all time. How, then, can Jesus say to His disciples *"a new commandment I give to you, that you love one another"* on the night before He died for us on the cross?

The Greek text uses a particular word for "new" that explains the answer to that question. John expresses Jesus' command with καινός as opposed to the synonym νέος. In many contexts, the two words for "new" are used interchangeably, but sometimes - as here - there is an important distinction. The word νέος emphasizes new with respect to time, new in reference to something that has recently come into existence. The word καινός emphasizes new with respect to quality. This is the word used in John 13:34. The emphasis is on new as opposed to something that has become worn out or damaged by age (TRE, p.220. A good example of this use is John 19:41. Joseph of Arimathea has a "new tomb" (καινός) in which no body had been laid. This was not a tomb that was new because it had been recently carved out of the rock. This was a new tomb in the sense that the tomb was fresh, never been used before. Here is the key to understanding the "new commandment." The new commandment to love one another is new in the sense of fresh, as opposed to the old commandment that had become worn out by usage. Jesus says, *"A fresh commandment I give to you, that you love one another."*

The freshness of the command to love one another rests on the foundation of a new standard for love and a new basis for love. The new basis for our love is the cross. We are to love with a "cross love." Jesus goes on to say that we are to love one another "as I have loved you." Here is the new standard for our love. The Mosaic Law commanded us to love our neighbors as ourselves. Loving another as I love myself is a high calling but a humanly doable calling. I can (sometimes!) attain to loving someone as I love myself. It is a fleshly standard - a human standard - for love, but at least it is humanly attainable. The fresh commandment for the new covenant is founded on the standard of Christ's love for us. Oh, how far I fall short of this standard for love! My only hope for loving others as Jesus loved me is to love others with His love. I cannot possibly love as He loved me unless He loves through me. Please Lord, love others through me - despite me - with your love!

HIS LOVE, OUR LOVE

Jesus loved us with a sacrificial love and commanded us to love each other with that same kind of love. He said, *"Just as I have loved you in order that you might also love each other"* (John 13:34). His love for us was highlighted by His sacrifice on the cross. Our love for each other is highlighted by our sacrifices for each other. The first word in the clause - "just as" (καθὼς) - provides the connection. He modeled the love He calls us to live. We are most like Him when we sacrifice for each other.

The contrast in verbal structure between His love and our love is instructive. When Jesus said, *"I have loved you,"* he used the indicative mode of expression in past time. This is the mode of fact. That He has loved us is a factual statement. Our love is expressed in the present tense and subjunctive mode (ἀγαπᾶτε). The present tense indicates ongoing, continuous love. We are to love one another with an ongoing love. Therein lies the challenge for it is easy to love another when all is going well in our relationships, but our love is to be an ongoing love even in the bad times. The subjunctive mode of expression is the mode of probability, not fact. Here the probability is connected to a command or expectation. We are not guaranteed to love as He loved, but we are expected to love as He loved.

As we unpack the verse more, we see that this is a purpose clause. Our love is introduced with the little word "in order that" (ἵνα). The purpose of His love for us is that we should love one another. He expects us to love each other because He loved us, and that is precisely why He loved us in the first place. The pronoun - "each other" (ἀλλήλοις) - is a reciprocal pronoun. The love he purposed for us is a reciprocal love between us. The next verse makes clear that the love Jesus is talking about here is among the disciples. We are to experience a reciprocal love by mutual expression.

Christians are known by our reciprocal love for each other as an ongoing habit of our lives. The purpose of Jesus' love for us is for us to love each other. He expects to see that love visible in us. When we fail to love each other, we fail to meet His expectations for us. Sadly, He suffers as much by our unloving actions in the church as He did by His loving sacrifice on the cross.

THE COMMUNITY OF JESUS

Love is the distinguishing mark of a follower of Jesus. Jesus said, *"By this, all will recognize that my disciples you are"* (John 13:35). The "my" (ἐμοὶ) is emphatic indicating that His name is at stake in our behavior. The clause "by this" (ἐν τούτῳ) refers to what follows not precedes the statement. The condition that follows identifies the mark of His followers. Jesus' followers are identifiable *"if you have love among yourselves."*

The clause is a third class condition sometimes called a "future more probable condition" (DM, p.290). There is an element of future uncertainty, but the uncertainty is outweighed by the expectation. This condition (ἐὰν ἀγάπην ἔχητε) indicates action that is expected or impending (BD, pp. 188-190). The same conditional structure is used in John 16:7 where Jesus says, *"If I do not go away, the Helper will not come to you; but if I go, I will send Him to you."* Obviously, Jesus' going is impending or expected. His going is only uncertain because it is yet future, but His going is expected. So is the love which marks us as Jesus' followers. Real followers of Jesus will love one another, not perfectly but actually. Jesus expected us to love one another and, we might say, is sadly "surprised" when we don't.

The "marking" love is a love we have among ourselves (ἐν ἀλλήλοις). Jesus is not thinking here of our love for those who are not followers of Jesus. Jesus says that the distinguishing mark is our love which is exercised within the community of believers (HAN, p.175). This is the love that He makes possible by changing our hearts by His grace. We should certainly love those in the world, but the real mark of a Christian is how we love other Christians. Sadly, we often do better at loving those outside the church than we do those inside the church. We reserve our harshest attacks for others who follow Jesus but deviate slightly from our expectations of orthodoxy or, more often orthopraxy - our personal practices! Our petty squabbles within the church turn vicious, grieving the heart of Jesus as we fail His expectations by dragging His name through the mud.

John 13:36-38

    Simon Peter said to him,
36 Λέγει αὐτῷ Σίμων Πέτρος·
        Lord, where are you going?
        Κύριε, ποῦ ὑπάγεις;
Jesus answered [him],
ἀπεκρίθη [αὐτῷ] Ἰησοῦς·
        where I am going, you are not able
        ὅπου ὑπάγω οὐ δύνασαί
            to follow me now,
            μοι νῦν ἀκολουθῆσαι,
            but you will follow me later.
            ἀκολουθήσεις δὲ ὕστερον.

    Peter said to him,
37 λέγει αὐτῷ ὁ Πέτρος·
        Lord,
        κύριε,
            because of what am I not able to follow you now?
            διὰ τί οὐ δύναμαί σοι ἀκολουθῆσαι ἄρτι;
            I will give up my life on behalf of you.
            τὴν ψυχήν μου ὑπὲρ σοῦ θήσω.
Jesus answered,
38 ἀποκρίνεται Ἰησοῦς·
        Will you give up your life on behalf of me?
        τὴν ψυχὴν σου ὑπὲρ ἐμοῦ θήσεις;
            Truly, truly I say to you,
            ἀμὴν ἀμὴν λέγω σοι,
                The cock will certainly not crow
                οὐ μὴ ἀλέκτωρ φωνήσῃ
                    until you disown me three times.
                    ἕως οὗ ἀρνήσῃ με τρίς.

JOHN 13

PREACHING POINTS

The conversational narrative revolves around two key statements made by Jesus, so there are two main preaching points. Each preaching point begins with the words of Peter but is defined by the teaching of Jesus. A blank line between verse 36 and 37 helps illustrate that the words of Peter in verse 37 introduce the response of Jesus in verse 38. The central idea should summarize both points.

Central Idea:

1. (v.36)

2. (vs. 37-38)

Briefly, identify two contemporary life parallels to these verses.

CLP #1

CLP #2

ABOUT CROWING COCKS AND PETER'S DENIALS

The prediction by Jesus that the "cock will not crow" (οὐ μὴ ἀλέκτωρ φωνήσῃ) until Peter denies Christ three times presents some problems of harmonization. All four gospels mention the cock crowing in fulfillment of Jesus' prophecy (Mt. 26:74; Jn. 18:27; Luke 22:60; Mk. 14:72). Mark records two cock-crowings (14:68 & 72). These biblical accounts present one of the more complex problems for harmonization in the gospels.

Did a rooster literally crow to signal Peter's denial?

Some have argued that the crowing of the rooster should not be understood literally. In this view, it is a reference to the signal ending the Roman watch known as "the cockcrow" (ἡ ἀλεκτοροφωνία). The timing of a crowing rooster would be an unpredictable event so the reference must be to a predictable time like the end of the third watch of the night (Mk. 13:35) when the "gallicinium" was sounded for the changing of the guard. The Roman guard observed four watches of the night. The third watch was called the cock crowing (ἀλεκτοροφωνία), and the fourth watch was called "the morning" (πρωΐ), so Peter would deny Christ multiple times before the fourth watch began. John uses the word πρωΐ in his account of what happened immediately after the cock crowing (Jn. 18:27-28), and it should be taken as a reference to the beginning of the fourth watch (BERN, 2:604).

There are several problems with this view. 1) The fulfillment accounts all describe a rooster crowing not a watchman's signal (MOR, p.635, fn79). John writes, *"immediately a cock crowed."* The text reads ἀλέκτωρ ἐφώνησεν not ἡ ἀλεκτοροφωνία as would be required for a reference to the watch. 2) The term, πρωΐ, (John 18:28) does not necessarily mean the morning watch. It is more commonly used as simply a reference to early in the morning. 3) The Jews, unlike the Romans, seemed to follow three night watches not four (MOR, p.760, fn55). Conclusion: The rooster crowed after Peter's denials. A crowing cock would have been a reminder to Peter throughout life of his failures and Christ's grace unlike the sound of the gallicinium which could only be heard if he was near a Roman garrison.

How many times did Jesus warn Peter about his coming denial?

All four gospels predict Peter's denial but in different times and places. Luke and John clearly present the prediction as taking place in the upper room (Lk. 22:34; Jn. 13:38) and before the group proceeded to the Mount of Olives (Lk.22:39; Jn. 18:1). Matthew and Mark record the prediction as taking place while the group was on the Mount of Olives (Mt. 26:34; Mk. 14:30). Some harmonize these accounts into one (ROB, p.194). Others see two promises and two predictions (CHE, p.185; TG, p.212).

Conclusion: Jesus predicted Peter's betrayal twice, first in the upper room and then again on the Mount of Olives for the following reasons. 1) The accounts take place in different locations. Mark and Matthew both place Peter's claim and the prediction as taking place after leaving the upper room (Mt. 26:34, cf. 26:30; Mk. 14:30, cf. 14:26). 2) The two prediction accounts differ in the details. In the first account, only Peter makes the bold claim, and only Peter is told of his coming prediction. In the second account, the disciples join Peter in making a bold claim never to deny Jesus after Jesus predicts Peter's denial (Mt. 26:35; Mk. 14:31). 3) The two prediction accounts picture Peter making two different claims. In the upper room, he promises to lay down his life for Jesus (Jn. 13:37). On the Mount of Olives, he promises he will never fall away from Jesus (Mt. 26:33).

Peter promises in the upper room to lay down his life for Jesus. Jesus predicts that Peter will deny him three times before the rooster crows. The disciples silently listen to the interchange between Jesus and Peter. Later, Peter promises never to fall away from Jesus. Jesus predicts that Peter will deny him three times before the rooster crows twice (Mk. 14:30). The disciples join Peter in professing their undying allegiance to Jesus. Peter's denials are doubly emphatic and doubly painful!

How many times did the rooster crow?

Matthew, Luke and John record that Peter denied Jesus before the rooster crowed. John 18:27 reads, "and immediately a rooster crowed" (καὶ εὐθέως ἀλέκτωρ ἐφώνησεν). The fulfillment matches the prediction in John 13:38 where Jesus says, "a cock shall not crow" (οὐ μὴ ἀλέκτωρ φωνήσῃ). The number of crowings is not mentioned in either case only the reality of a crowing. Mark, alone, records that the rooster would crow and did crow twice. According to Mark, Jesus predicted that Peter would deny Him before "a rooster crows twice" (πρὶν ἢ δὶς ἀλέκτορα φωνῆσαι) in Mark 14:30. Then Mark recorded that "a cock crowed a second time" (ἐκ δευτέρου ἀλέκτωρ ἐφώνησεν) after Peter betrayed Jesus (Mark 14:72). Peter remembered that Jesus predicted that the rooster would crow twice (δὶς) before Peter denied him three times (δὶς τρίς με ἀπαρνήσῃ). The positioning of the numbers (δὶς τρίς) side by side calls attention to the double crowing so that there can be no mistake about Mark's intention.

Some argue that this is a contradiction. Mark's record must be a mistake – a variant - because John does not accept his record of two crowings (BERN, 2:529-530). Others argue that the cock crowed twice and Mark is the only one who recorded that tidbit of information (CHE, p.218). Conclusion: the rooster crowed twice that morning. Mark is more specific than John and the other writers in recording that the second crowing precipitated Peter's tears. Mark's repetition of the number is striking and cannot be dismissed easily as a mistake. The other gospel writers are more generic. They do not deny a second cock-crowing. They merely fail to mention that detail. It is possible that there were normally two cock-crowings, an early and a later one, as some speculate (TG, p.220). There is no contradiction because the accounts can be easily harmonized. Peter's denial of Jesus is even more dramatic when we realize that the rooster crowed twice, first in ominous warning and second as an indictment. No wonder he wept!

How many times did Peter deny Jesus?

The popular understanding is that Peter denied Jesus three times before the rooster crowed that morning. The reason for the common interpretation of three denials is that Jesus predicted three denials. However, the prediction does not necessarily exclude more denials, only that there would be at least three denials (TG, p.229). Some have argued for as many as six denials, three before each crowing of the rooster (CHE, pp.218ff). The argument is that John's prediction of three denials (John 18:38) and Mark's prediction of three denials (Mark 14:30) are two separate warnings because of the differences in the language. John calls attention to the warning that the rooster will not crow at all (οὐ μὴ) before Peter denies Jesus three times. The emphatic "not, never" means that the rooster would not even crow the first time before three denials took place. Mark records Jesus' warning that Peter would deny him three times before the rooster crowed twice. The result is that there were three denials before the first crowing and three before the second crowing. Later manuscripts add a first cock crowing in Mark 14:68 after some early denials in support of this argument (CHE, p.219).

Conclusion: All four Gospels record three denials to demonstrate that Peter fulfilled the prophecy of Jesus, but John records one of his denials taking place in the courtyard of Annas before Jesus was transported to the home of Caiaphas leading to the conclusion that Peter denied Jesus at least four times (TG, p.229). There is overlap in the accounts recorded by the four writers, so it seems unlikely that there were six denials. The attempt to identify six denials (CHE, p.219) is strained by the artificial intention to find three denials for each cock crowing, and the double negative in John 13:38 (οὐ μὴ) does not require an interpretation of "not, ever." The double negative can be used for emphasis.

Therefore, I think it is best to see at least four and probably five denials by Peter that night.

First Denial – John 18:17
    courtyard of Annas
Second Denial – John 18:25
    first servant girl by the fire in the courtyard of Caiaphas (cf. Mt. 26:70; Mk. 14:68; Lk. 22:57)
Third Denial – Matthew 26:71-72
    "another" servant girl (maid) by the fire (cf. Mk. 14:69-70)
Fourth Denial – Luke 22:58
    an unnamed man by the fire with other bystanders (cf. Mt. 26:74; Mk. 14:71; Lk. 22:60)
Fifth Denial – John 18:27
    a relative of the man whose ear Peter cut off (perhaps one of the bystanders)

Peter denied Jesus and was warned by the first cock-crowing, but he continued to deny Jesus until the second cock-crowing. An accurate understanding of the story makes Peter's denial more heinous and Christ's grace more gracious!

JOHN 14

John 14:1-3

Do not allow your heart to be agitated,
Μὴ ταρασσέσθω ὑμῶν ἡ καρδία·
> You are trusting in God
> πιστεύετε εἰς τὸν θεὸν
> trust also in me.
> καὶ εἰς ἐμὲ πιστεύετε.

In my Father's house are many living places
2 ἐν τῇ οἰκίᾳ τοῦ πατρός μου μοναὶ πολλαί εἰσιν·
> If not, I would have told you
> εἰ δὲ μή, εἶπον ἂν ὑμῖν
because I am going to prepare a place for you. (statement not question)
ὅτι πορεύομαι ἑτοιμάσαι τόπον ὑμῖν;

> And If I go
> 3 καὶ ἐὰν πορευθῶ
> And prepare a place for you,
> καὶ ἑτοιμάσω τόπον ὑμῖν,
I will come again
πάλιν ἔρχομαι
and I will take you to myself,
καὶ παραλήμψομαι ὑμᾶς πρὸς ἐμαυτόν,
> that where I, myself, am
> ἵνα ὅπου εἰμὶ ἐγὼ
> you, yourselves, also might be.
> καὶ ὑμεῖς ἦτε.

JOHN 14

PREACHING POINTS

There are three main preaching points, the command not to be agitated, the home being prepared and the welcoming return of Jesus. Notice that I have translated the preparation as a statement, not a question despite the punctuation mark the editors have supplied. The statement changes the emphasis giving a reason for the promise. The central idea should summarize the three main preaching points.

Central Idea:

1. (v.1)

2. (v.2)

3. (v.3)

Briefly, identify two contemporary life parallels to these verses.

CLP #1

CLP #2

ARE YOU EVER AGITATED?

Jesus commands us, *"Do not let your heart be troubled"* (John 14:1). The word "troubled" means to be stirred up like waters muddied by the tramping of many feet as it is used in the Greek translation of Ezekiel 32:2, 13 (Septuagint). To be troubled is to be agitated, unsettled or thrown into mental confusion. The present imperative with a negative commands us to stop an action already in process (Μὴ ταρασσέσθω). Jesus is specifically addressing Peter's question, *"Lord, why can I not follow you"* (John 13:37). The disciples were already troubled and needed to stop being agitated (RIEN, p. 251).

Why does Jesus command them (and by extension us) to stop letting themselves be troubled when even Jesus was troubled? The same word is used to describe Jesus only minutes earlier on that very night (John 13:21) and at the death of His friend Lazarus (John 11:33). How can Jesus command us to stop being troubled when He was troubled?

First, Jesus was troubled that night by the presence of Judas, the betrayer, in the Upper Room (13:21) because it hindered the intimacy of His final night. Jesus resolved that troubling after Judas left the room and Jesus could proceed to teach His disciples without the betrayer present (13:31). The departure of Judas relieved Jesus' spirit, so he stopped being troubled just as he commands us to stop being troubled. It is not sin to be troubled, but we must not allow the troubling to continue. Second, this is a passive verb meaning that outside circumstances trouble us. When Jesus was troubled at the death of Lazarus (11:33), an active verb is used indicating that He troubled Himself (ἐτάραξεν ἑαυτὸν). There are times when we should trouble ourselves just as Jesus did. All "troubling" is not bad troubling! Some events like death or sin should disturb us. They disturbed Jesus!

Finally, the command here is a present tense command indicating a continuous, ongoing disturbance as opposed to the use of the Aorist to indicate something simply happened (11:33; 13:21). The prohibition against allowing ourselves to be agitated by our circumstances is the forbidding of a habit or an ongoing practice. Stop letting yourselves be troubled by your circumstances as an ongoing practice in your life!

We all, just like Jesus, become agitated. It is part of the human experience. Sometimes we should become disturbed by what we experience in life. However, we should not allow ourselves to be agitated by our circumstances on a continual, habitual basis. Such continuous agitation is destructive. The antidote is faith as Jesus makes clear in the next phrase. We should not allow ourselves to be thrown into confusion by our circumstances. The antidote to confusion is truth as Jesus makes clear in the following verses. We must trust God and know His truth to avoid the troubling that we must not allow in our lives.

WHO DO YOU BELIEVE?

The opening verses of John 14 are among the most familiar, precious and comforting verses in the Bible. I hesitate to disturb our familiarity with questions about the text, yet significant questions are raised by the text. One of those questions pertains to the translation of "believe" or "trust" in verse one.

Jesus uses the word "believe" (πιστεύετε) twice. Jesus says, *"Believe in God, believe also in Me"* (NASB). Or does He say, *"Ye believe in God, believe also in Me"* (KJV)? Or perhaps Jesus says, *"Believe in God, you are believing in Me"*? Or is it, *"You are believing in God, you are believing in Me"* (Luther)? All four translations are grammatically possible (MEY, pp. 406-407). Which translation accurately expresses the thought of Jesus?

The form of the verb "believe" (πιστεύετε) is ambiguous. There are four ways these verbs could be translated. 1) Both verbs are imperatives (commands). 2) The first verb is an indicative (statement of fact) and the second is a command. 3) The first verb is a command and the second is a statement. 4) Both verbs are indicatives making factual statements. It is a matter of interpretation since all four translations are grammatically correct. The question boils down to the precise point that Jesus is making in this verse.

Many argue that Jesus was commanding both faith in God and faith in Him. The two verbs should be translated the same way according to many. However, I think that Jesus recognized they had faith in God already, but they needed to trust Him. I think that Jesus said, *"You trust (statement of fact) in God, trust (command) in Me also"* (HBM). He had just predicted that He is leaving the disciples and that Peter would deny Him three times before the cock crowed. These are troubling predictions that raise doubts about what Jesus is doing. Jesus was not commanding them to believe God. They were pious Israelites. He knew they believed God. Jesus was commanding them to trust Him. After all, He was the one troubling them with these predictions.

For the Christian, trusting Jesus personally is inseparable from trusting God. Trusting Jesus personally is essential to being a Christian - a unique mark of a Christian. Many believe God. Many are religious. Many populate our churches. Many claim to be Christian. Yet no one is a Christian who fails to trust Christ for no one comes the Father but through the Son (14:6)!

BELIEVE IN ME!

Why command believers to believe?

Jesus was speaking to His disciples in the Upper Room when He commanded them to *"believe also in Me"* (John 14:1). These were men who were already believers - every one of them! Judas, the betrayer, has left the room. Only believers remain, yet Jesus ordered them to believe. Why?

The answer is found in the tense of the verb "believe" (πιστεύετε). This is a present tense verb. The present tense emphasizes continuing faith - ongoing faith - no matter what comes. They could not know the crucible they were being thrown into in the next few hours. The fires of hell would soon test their faith. We too cannot know the severe tests that will search our faith, and we must obey the command to continue to believe no matter what comes. True faith is persevering faith.

A saving faith is a growing faith. Jesus says, *"Believe in Me"* (εἰς ἐμὲ). The "in me" is emphatic. The preposition (εἰς) indicates motion towards a person or thing. There is a sense of movement in real faith. We are not merely convinced that the teachings of Jesus are true or that he lived in history. We are moving into a deepening sense of His nearness to help and His power to meet our needs.

"There is a faith that accepts the words spoken and a faith that accepts the person who speaks. The former is only part of the latter" (SLJ).

We are growing to trust Him not just His words. We trust His character not just His teachings. We trust His love not just His doctrine. We trust He will never let us down even when we don't know how He will hold us up.

ASSURANCE OF HEAVEN

Jesus gives heavenly assurance when He speaks of *"My Father's house"* - a familiar expression for heaven (John 14:2). Philo, the Jewish philosopher, wrote of a soul returning "into the father's house," meaning heaven (BERN, 2:531). Jesus assures us that He is going (futuristic present) to prepare a place for us in His Father's house. Sandwiched between the opening phrase, *"in My Father's house,"* and the closing assurance, *"to prepare a place,"* is a clause that requires some attention.

The clause - *"if it were not so, I would have have told you"* - can be translated as either a question or a statement. As a question, it reads, *"If it were not so would I have told you that I go to prepare a place for you?"* (ESV, NIV) As a statement, it reads, *"If it were not so I would have told you, for I go to prepare a place for you."* (NASB, KJV) There were no punctuation marks in the original manuscripts, so either translation is possible. The interpretation hinges on the little word, ὅτι, which can be translated either as "that" or "for/because." If we translate ὅτι as "that," we will read the clause as a question. If we translate ὅτι as "because," we will read the clause as a statement.

I don't think we should understand the clause as a question because Jesus never told them before that He was going to prepare a place for them so the question would be meaningless. I think it is best to understand ὅτι as "because" making the preceding clause parenthetical. I connect the final clause - *"because I go to prepare a place for you"* - with the first clause - *"in My Father's house are many dwelling places"* - making the middle clause a parenthesis. There are many rooms in heaven because He is going to prepare them for us.

"In My Father's house, there are many rooms (but if not, I would have told you) because I am going to prepare a place for you."

Jesus reassures us that there is room in heaven for us or He would have warned us not to expect a room in heaven. He left earth to prepare a place for us in heaven. The word "place" (τόπον) meant a room to live, stay or sit (BAGD). The word "to prepare" (ἑτοιμάσαι) was commonly used for preparations made for someone coming to visit (MM, p.258). Jesus is preparing our rooms for our homecoming much like a parent prepares the room of a child coming home from college. Our assurance is that Jesus would have warned us not to expect a homecoming if this was not true.

Praise God for the promise of our homecoming!

HEAVENLY CONDOS!

Where will we live in heaven? Jesus is preparing a place for us, but what will that place be like? He tells us, *"In My Father's house are many mansions"* (John 14:2). Do we have mansions awaiting us in heaven? What can we expect to enjoy in our heavenly homes?

Origen, one of the early Church Fathers, taught that when a person died, he or she first lived in a place called "Paradise" to be instructed properly before entering heaven. Then the saint, once instructed, ascended through a series of mansions or stations ("halting places") on his or her way to God. The mansions were stages that saints passed through on their way to glory according to Origen (BERN, 2:532). Death was the beginning of a journey to heaven that passed through many tarrying places.

Origen's interpretation flies in the face of what we know about the meaning of this word and other Scripture that promises us immediate entry into heaven (2 Corinthians 5:8). The Greek word is μοναί which means abiding places, abodes, rooms or dwelling places not stages of life (BAGD, p. 527). The Latin word *"mansio"* and the old English word *"mansion"* meant a dwelling place, not a palatial residence as we use the word today. The Jews believed that heaven had many compartments where people lived (NIDNTT, 3:229). These compartments corresponded to the degrees of reward earned through life on earth. The early Church Father, Irenaeus, citing the "Elders," used John 14:2 to suggest that the dwelling places in heaven corresponded to the thirty, sixty and hundredfold harvests in the Parable of the Sower (Matthew 13:23). Clement of Alexandria taught that the dwelling places in heaven were given to saints according to their service on earth (BERN, 2:532).

The best way to understand the word is to see heaven as a condominium complex with many rooms, suites or apartments. These are permanent residences, not temporary motels we pass through on our journey. Jesus is telling us that heaven is one house (οἰκία) with many apartments (μοναὶ πολλαί). The only other place in the New Testament where this word is used is a few verses later in John 14:23. Jesus said, *"If anyone loves Me, he will keep My word; and My Father will love him, and We will come to him and make our abode (μονὴν) with him."* This is clearly a permanent residence - a home - not a temporary tarrying place nor a stage in a journey.

Heaven is one giant condominium complex with many suites or apartments where we shall rest after our long journey on earth. Jesus has gone to prepare a place for us in the Grand Condominiums of Heaven! These heavenly "condos" are not open wards but individual suites designed for each of us as our permanent abiding places in heaven. God loves us individually not just collectively!

HE'S COMING BACK!

Jesus made an important promise to us on His last night before the crucifixion. He said, *"If I go and prepare a place for you, I will come again and receive you to myself"* (John 14:3). This wonderful promise has comforted believers through many trials throughout history. What exactly did Jesus mean by His promise?

Christians have understood this promise in a number of ways. (1) Jesus promises a spiritual coming at every trial, but when did He ever leave them spiritually? (2) Jesus promises to come to them in the resurrection, but how does He receive them to Himself at the Resurrection? (3) Jesus promises to come to them in the coming of the Holy Spirit on the Day of Pentecost, but how is this a coming "again" and how does He receive them to Himself at that time? (4) Jesus promises to come to believers - including us - when we die, but that is usually presented in the Bible as our going to Him (Phil. 1:23; 2 Cor. 5:8). None of these views satisfactorily explains what Jesus promises.

Jesus promises us (believers down through history) that He will come again to earth from heaven. This is the hope of every Christian and the correct understanding of His promise for the following reasons. (1) The use of "again" (πάλιν) points back to a first coming. The first coming was bodily not spiritually and on earth not in heaven, so the second coming must be the same. (2) The coming and receiving are grammatically parallel to the going and preparing. If "I go" then "I will come again"! He is leaving them bodily not spiritually, so the coming must be bodily not spiritually. *"If I prepare a place for you"* then *"I will receive you to myself."* The prepared place is heaven so the reception must be in heaven. (3) Jesus speaks elsewhere of coming again with reference to His bodily return (John 14:28; 21:22).

Jesus uses a present tense form of the verb to describe His return (ἔρχομαι) to make the promise more vivid and exciting. It is a futurist present (BD, p. 168) because the receiving is in the future tense (παραλήμψομαι). *"I am coming again, and I will receive you to myself."* Jesus promises to come to us on earth to receive us in heaven - His prepared place. His coming again is to escort us back to heaven with Him. We call this event the "Rapture, " and we are to comfort each other with His promise (1 Thessalonians 4:16-18).

John 14:4-7

You also know the way where I am going.
4 καὶ ὅπου [ἐγὼ] ὑπάγω οἴδατε τὴν ὁδόν.
    Thomas said to him,
    5 Λέγει αὐτῷ Θωμᾶς·
        Lord, we do not know where you are going
        κύριε, οὐκ οἴδαμεν ποῦ ὑπάγεις·
        how are we able to know the way?
        πῶς δυνάμεθα τὴν ὁδὸν εἰδέναι;
    Jesus said to him,
    6 λέγει αὐτῷ [ὁ] Ἰησοῦς·

I, myself, am the way
ἐγώ εἰμι ἡ ὁδὸς

and the truth
καὶ ἡ ἀλήθεια

and the life
καὶ ἡ ζωή·
    no one comes to the Father
    οὐδεὶς ἔρχεται πρὸς τὸν πατέρα
        except through me.
        εἰ μὴ δι᾽ ἐμοῦ.
        If you had known me,
        7 εἰ ἐγνώκατέ με,
            You also would have known my father.
            καὶ τὸν πατέρα μου γνώσεσθε.
                And from just now you know Him
                καὶ ἀπ᾽ ἄρτι γινώσκετε αὐτὸν
                and you have seen Him.
                καὶ ἑωράκατε αὐτόν.

JOHN 14

PREACHING POINTS

The statement of Jesus ending verse four is often taken with the previous section. However, the statement about knowing the way serves as a good introduction to Jesus' answer to Philip in this section. The purpose of the structural diagram is to picture the main ideas of the text grammatically. The focus is on the way to where Jesus is going, not on the place where Jesus is going. The conversation between Thomas and Jesus merely introduces the answer, so their conversation is not the main idea. There are three main preaching points corresponding to the classic threefold answer that Jesus gave describing how to get where he was going. The central idea should summarize these three points.

Central Idea:

1. (v.6a)

2. (v.6b)

3. (v.6c)

Briefly, identify two contemporary life parallels to these verses.

CLP #1

CLP #2

I AM!

Jesus said, *"I am the way and the truth and the life"* (John 14:6). The "I" (ἐγώ) is emphatic - "I, myself, am." The verb is a present tense verb indicating continuous action or a state of existence. The two words together (ἐγώ εἰμι) form an affirmation of eternal existence pointing back to the great "I Am" of the Old Testament (Exodus 3:14).

Jesus makes three claims connected by the conjunction καί. Each one has the definite article. Jesus claims to be *"the way"* (ἡ ὁδός), *"the truth"* (ἡ ἀλήθεια) and *"the life"* (ἡ ζωή). An article is commonly attached to an abstract noun in order to point back to what has already been mentioned. This is called an "anaphoric" use of the article. The article in *"the way"* fits the anaphoric use because Jesus is answering the question by Thomas in the previous verse. The article points back to that question. However, the other two articles cannot be anaphoric since there is nothing in the context about "truth" and "life." What do these articles tell us about Jesus in this classic assertion of Christianity?

The verb εἰμι is an equative verb. The three assertions are predicate nominatives. An article is used with a predicate nominative to assert that the subject and the predicate nominative are identical. The verb equates the subject with the predicate nominative. The article specifies that the subject and predicate nominative are "convertible" (ATR, p. 768).

I = way and way = I
I = truth and truth = I
I = life and life = I

Jesus makes three radical claims. He, personally, is the only way to the Father as the next clause makes clear. Jesus also claims that he, personally, is the essence of truth and the embodiment of life. "I am the only way to the Father because truth and life are wrapped up in me personally! To know me is to know truth and experience life on the way to the Father!" What man can make that claim without being considered cuckoo?

KNOWING JESUS

John 14:7 can be translated in two very different ways because of a textual problem. (1) *"If you had known Me, you would have known My Father also"* (ESV). (2) *"If you really knew me, you will know my Father as well"* (NIV). The first version is a rebuke and the second is a promise. Is Jesus rebuking them for not knowing him as they should have known him or is Jesus promising them that they will know the father because they already know the son?

The protasis (condition) is essentially the same in both cases (minor textual differences), but the apodosis (result) has a major textual problem. The form of the apodosis determines the nature of the protasis. (1) *"You would have known* (αν ἤδειτε) *my Father."* The condition becomes a contrary to fact condition rebuking them for not knowing him as they should have known him. (2) *"You will know* (γνώσεσθε) *my Father."* In this case, the condition is assumed to be true resulting in a promise that they will know the father based on what Jesus said in verse 6. The manuscript evidence is strong for both forms of the text.

I take it to be a rebuke. *"If you had known me, you would have known my Father also."* There are two reasons for this conclusion. (1) Jesus made the same statement in John 8:19 to the Jews in the temple. They did not know Jesus so they could not know his father. (2) This translation is consistent with the rebuke Jesus gives to Philip in John 14:9. Philip immediately proved he did not really know Jesus by his question (v.8), so Jesus rebuked him for his lack of knowledge.

The conditional sentence implies that the disciples have not really known Jesus so have not known God the Father. They knew Jesus on one level. They walked, talked and worked with him. On another level, they did not yet know him so did not really know the father because to really know Jesus is to know the Father. To know Christ means that we know him in such a way that the knowledge changes how we live like knowing a spouse in the fullest sense changes how we relate to everyone else. Our knowledge changes the choices we make in life. So, knowing Jesus changes how we live, and this level of knowledge is the only way to know God as Father.

TO SEE GOD

The statement is shockingly simple yet infinitely profound. *"From now on (ἀπ' ἄρτι) you know Him (God) and you have seen Him"* (John 14:7). You all (plural) know God now (γινώσκετε). The present tense indicative verb emphasizes continuing knowledge from this point onward. You all have seen God (ἑωράκατε). The perfect tense indicative verb emphasizes past action that stands accomplished in the present (BUR, p.40). Jesus expands His thought with two more perfect tense verbs in response to Philip's question. *"The one who has seen me has seen the Father"* (John 14:9). It is not that they will see God. They have seen God - in Jesus. Jesus makes a staggering claim.

There are two Greek words often used for sight. Βλέπω means to see in terms of the physical senses or as an intellectual function of paying attention. The word used here, ὁράω, refers to spiritual perception (BAGD, p.578). John uses ὁράω for what the Son in His preexistence saw when He was with the Father in eternity past (John 3:11, 32; 6:46; 8:38; NIDNTT, 3:515-517). No one else has seen the Father - until now, Jesus asserts! The Bible teaches that God is invisible (Col. 1:15; 1 Tim. 1:17). The word is a verbal adjective related to ὁράω with the alpha negative added (α - ορατος). Moses "saw" God in the Old Testament but it was a theophany - a manifestation of God (Ex. 33:13,18). Jesus now claims that the disciples have seen God in a way that Moses never did precisely because they have seen Jesus.

How have they seen God? John uses the word for seeing by faith (John 12:45). The believer perceives the Father in the Son. The unbeliever does not. I like what John Baillie said, "Through God alone can God be known!" Jesus is not saying here that He represents the Father or is the Father's ambassador to humans. You cannot know someone through knowing someone who knows him. Jesus claims that you know the Father when you know the Son. He claims that when you see Jesus, you have seen the invisible God!

John 14:8-11

    Philip said to him,
8 Λέγει αὐτῷ Φίλιππος·
        Lord, Show to us the Father, and it is sufficient for us.
        Κύριε, δεῖξον ἡμῖν τὸν πατέρα, καὶ ἀρκεῖ ἡμῖν.
    Jesus said to him,
9 λέγει αὐτῷ ὁ Ἰησοῦς·
        Am I so much time with you and you have not come to know me, Philip?
        τοσούτῳ χρόνῳ μεθ' ὑμῶν εἰμι καὶ οὐκ ἔγνωκάς με, Φίλιππε;
The one who has seen me has seen the Father,
ὁ ἑωρακὼς ἐμὲ ἑώρακεν τὸν πατέρα·
        How can you say, show us the Father?
        πῶς σὺ λέγεις· δεῖξον ἡμῖν τὸν πατέρα;

    Do you not believe
10 οὐ πιστεύεις
        That I, myself, (am) in the Father
        ὅτι ἐγὼ ἐν τῷ πατρὶ
        and the Father is in me?
        καὶ ὁ πατὴρ ἐν ἐμοί ἐστιν;

    The words which I, myself, say to you
    τὰ ῥήματα ἃ ἐγὼ λέγω ὑμῖν
        from myself, I do not say,
        ἀπ' ἐμαυτοῦ οὐ λαλῶ,
            But the father
            ὁ δὲ πατὴρ
                remaining in me
                ἐν ἐμοὶ μένων
            is doing his works.
            ποιεῖ τὰ ἔργα αὐτοῦ.

    Believe in me
11 πιστεύετέ μοι
        That I, myself, (am) in the Father and the Father in me,
        ὅτι ἐγὼ ἐν τῷ πατρὶ καὶ ὁ πατὴρ ἐν ἐμοί·
    but if not,
    εἰ δὲ μή,
    believe because of the works themselves.
    διὰ τὰ ἔργα αὐτὰ πιστεύετε.

JOHN 14

PREACHING POINTS

The main point of the section is found in verse 9. Jesus makes His vital theological assertion in answer to Philip's question. Jesus then gives three arguments for His assertion that anyone who sees Jesus sees the Father. The first argument is in the form of a question. The second is an explanation, and the third is a call to believe.

Central Idea: (v.9)

1. (v.10a)

2. (v.10b)

3. (v.11)

Briefly, identify two contemporary life parallels to these verses.

CLP #1

CLP #2

SATISFIED WITH GOD

What does it take for us to be satisfied with God? How does God prove His sufficiency to us? When is God enough for us? Philip raises these kinds of questions in John 14:8-9. He defines his requirement for contentment with God when he says, *"Lord, show us the Father, and it is enough for us."*

The verb translated "it is enough" (ἀρκεῖ) means to be sufficient, to be satisfied or content with something or someone (BAGD, p.107). The word is commonly used as an admonition to be content with God's provision rather than becoming complacent with human success. The Jewish Rabbis exhorted the people to be satisfied with God's guidance and grace. The Rabbinic paraphrase of Genesis 17:1 reads, "Then spake the Holy One, blessed be He: Abraham, be content that I am thy God, be content that I am thy Protector" (TDNT, 1:466).

Knowing God by faith should be enough for us, but it isn't always. We, like Philip, say, show me! The verb translated "show" (δεῖξον) is a command – a demand of Jesus. Philip is not so different from the Pharisees here (Jn.8:19). The verb means to show in the sense of exhibit or prove something (TDNT, 2:25). Jesus told the leper He healed to show (δεῖξον) himself to the priest (Mt. 8:4). Philip may well have had in mind a theophany like Moses saw (Ex. 24:9-10) and asked to see (Ex. 33:18). Philip wanted to see a revelation of God (MEY, 3:411) – proof of His glory. We too want proof of God's glory before we are content with His grace.

Jesus responded to Philip with a force that comes out better in a woodenly literal translation. "So much time with you I am being, and you have not known Me, Philip?" The verb translated "I have been" is a present tense verb meaning "I am being" (εἰμι). It could be a perfective present, but those are rare. It is likely a progressive present speaking of action in the past up to the present and continuing in progress as Jesus is speaking (MHT, 3:62). Jesus' presence with Philip should have been enough for Philip.

We enjoy the greatest satisfaction with God when experiencing the gracious presence of Jesus in our daily lives. God's sufficiency is not found in the spectacular display of His glory but in the perfection of His power in our weakness. Paul uses the same word to describe his experience when Jesus told him, *"My grace is sufficient (ἀρκεῖ) for you for in weakness power is perfected"* (2 Cor. 12:9).

Lord, you are enough for me. I need no other proof than your daily presence in my life.

UNION AND INTIMACY

The union of the Father and the Son is proved by Jesus' words and the Father's works (John 14:10). Jesus proves that He is in the Father because He does not speak on His own initiative. He does not speak "by means of Himself" (ἀπ' ἐμαυτοῦ). The Father proves that Jesus does not speak on His own initiative by the works God does through Jesus. The works verify the words.

The Father is living in Jesus (John 14:10). The word "living" (μένων) is a nominative participle modifying Father. It means enduring, continuing or remaining. The Father is continuously living in

Jesus. Jesus says, "The living in me Father" performs (ποιεῖ) - on an ongoing basis - His works, thereby verifying the words of Jesus.

Jesus calls us to believe Him (John 14:11). What are we to believe? Jesus defines the content of our faith not the cause of our faith in the expression *"I am in the Father, and the Father is in Me."* The particle (ὅτι) should be translated "that" not "because" (Meyer, *John*, p 412). We are to believe Jesus when He says *"that I am in the Father and the Father is in Me."* This is an essential doctrine of Christianity.

Why must we believe that? We must believe Jesus' words about His union with the Father because the mutual indwelling of the Father and the Son is the foundation for the mutual indwelling of Jesus and His followers (John 14:20). We are in Jesus, and Jesus is in us. Jesus is in the Father, and the Father is in Jesus. The Father sends the Spirit of Truth to be in us (John 14:17). The Tri-Unity of God is the model for our unity in Jesus, so the Tri-Unity of God is an essential teaching of our faith.

The basis of our union with Jesus is His union with the Father. We must believe His union with the Father in order to experience our union with Jesus. The intimacy we enjoy with Jesus is grounded in the intimacy He enjoys with the Father.

John 14:12-14

Truly, truly I say to you,
12 Ἀμὴν ἀμὴν λέγω ὑμῖν,

    The one who believes in me
    ὁ πιστεύων εἰς ἐμὲ
        The works which I, myself, am doing
        τὰ ἔργα ἃ ἐγὼ ποιῶ
            and also he will do
            κἀκεῖνος ποιήσει
    and greater than these he will do,
    καὶ μείζονα τούτων ποιήσει,
        because I am going to the Father,
        ὅτι ἐγὼ πρὸς τὸν πατέρα πορεύομαι·

    and whatever you might ask
13 καὶ ὅ τι ἂν αἰτήσητε
        In my name
        ἐν τῷ ὀνόματί μου
    this I will do,
    τοῦτο ποιήσω,
        in order that the Father might be glorified
        ἵνα δοξασθῇ ὁ πατὴρ
            in the Son.
            ἐν τῷ υἱῷ.
    If you ask me anything
14 ἐάν τι αἰτήσητέ με
        In my name
        ἐν τῷ ὀνόματί μου
    I, myself, will do.
    ἐγὼ ποιήσω.

JOHN 14

PREACHING POINTS

There are two main preaching points. The first has to do with works and the second with prayer. The central idea of the message would tie these two points together into a single summary principle.

Central Idea:

1. (v.12)

2. (vs.13-14)

Briefly, identify two contemporary life parallels to these verses.

CLP #1

CLP #2

GREATER WORKS!

Miracles to us are mere works to Jesus. The works (ἔργα) Jesus did on earth often referred to miraculous deeds (John 5:20; 7:21) that no one else ever did (John 15:24). However, all of these works were part of one great work - the work Jesus came to do on earth - to save mankind (John 17:4). Jesus considered this work His greatest work. "Works" are "a way of linking the miracles with the non-miraculous. It shows the whole of Jesus life glowed with divine glory" (MOR, p.689) as He worked out His salvation purpose.

Jesus said, *"He who believes in Me, the works (εργα) that I do, he will do also; and greater than these he will do; because I go to the Father"* (John 14:12). One of the proofs validating Jesus' claims is the fact that His followers do greater works than He did. The particle ὅτι is causal. His followers will do (ποιήσει) greater works because Jesus goes to the Father. The departure of Jesus causes greater works to be done through His followers - by extension, us!

How did the disciples do greater (μείζονα) works than Jesus? Jesus healed the sick and raised the dead. How can our works be greater than those works? The Apostles certainly did some great miracles. People were healed when Peter's shadow fell on them (Acts 5:12-16), and God healed people by the sweat rags of Paul (Acts 19:11-12). Sadly, many today try to emulate these miraculous works not understanding that Jesus was talking about greater works than these. The comparative adjective requires a standard of measurement to apply to the comparison.

Our works are greater in power because they are done by God using weak, flawed and sinful humans. God chooses to get His work done through us requiring greater power than if He had done it Himself. When all is said and done, the works we do are ultimately His works done through us. That anyone in this world should be drawn to Jesus through our soiled works is an act of omnipotence!

Our works are greater in scope. Jesus left this world having accumulated 500 disciples after three years of work. Peter preached one sermon, and 3,000 people were saved. The works of Jesus have been expanded exponentially into a global kingdom by the followers of Jesus. Works expanded are greater works.

Our works are greater in value. Jesus implied that His spiritual works were greater than His physical miracles (John 5:20) showing us that spiritual conversion is more valuable to Jesus than physical healing. There is no greater work in the mind of Jesus than the conversion of one soul. Jesus does His conversion work through us thereby using us to do greater works for Him. The miracle of conversion is the greatest work of all!

ANYTHING WE ASK??!

Jesus makes a staggering promise to do what we ask in John 14:13-14. *"Whatever (ὅ τι ἂν) you ask in my name that I will do, so that the Father may be glorified in the Son. If you ask me anything (ἐάν τι) in my name, I will do it."* Will Jesus do anything we ask? What if I ask for the opposite of what you ask? Will He do what I ask or what you ask?

Jesus does not promise to do anything I ask Him to do. What He promises to do is whatever I ask as long as what I ask meets two criteria in this verse. The basis of my request must be *"in Jesus name"* (ἐν τῷ ὀνόματί μου). The purpose of my request must be to glorify the Father through the Son's answer (ἵνα δοξασθῇ). When I align my request with His basis and His purpose, He will do whatever I ask, but He does not promise to do what does not align with His basis and His purpose.

The basis for my request must always be *"in Jesus name."* Many suggest that prayer in Jesus name means on the merits of what Jesus has accomplished for us. However, the same phrase is used in John 14:26 where the Father will send the Holy Spirit "in my name" (ἐν τῷ ὀνόματί μου). Does the Father send the Holy Spirit on the merits of what Jesus has done for us? Perhaps, but I think there is a better sense for the phrase.

The better understanding of asking in Jesus name is that we are asking God to do something on the basis that Jesus is our representative before the Father. The Father sends the Holy Spirit to us on the basis that Jesus represents us to the Father. Jesus is in the Father. We are in Jesus, and Jesus is in us (John 14:20). Because of that representative relationship we can ask whatever we want. Prayer "in Jesus name" is not a magic formula but the expression of an intimate union with Jesus. Our union with Him frames our request to Him. Whatever we ask will be aligned with whatever He wants because we enjoy an intimate friendship with Him.

The purpose of our request is the glory of God. We ask whatever we want in order to see the Father glorified in the Son when the Son answers our request. We don't pray for our wants but for His honor. Our requests must be aligned with His glory, or the promise is mitigated. When we are so in tune with Jesus that what we want most glorifies the Son, then we can ask whatever we want, and He will do it for us.

The closer I am to Jesus; the more intimately I know Him; the more likely I am to ask for what He most wants to do just like any love relationship. The more I seek what will honor Him, the more He seeks to do what I ask. Sadly, and all too often, what I ask for uses Him to meet my goals instead of to seek His glory. Prayer is a request between close friends not a requisition from a business partner.

TO WHOM SHOULD WE PRAY?

The normal pattern for prayer in the New Testament is to the Father through the Son. We ask the Father to answer our prayers on the basis of our relationship with the Son. Some try to make this pattern into a rigid formula for prayer despite the fact that Stephen prayed directly to Jesus pleading on behalf of those who stoned him to death (Acts 7:59-60).

Jesus promised, *"Whatever you ask in My name, that I will do, so that the Father may be glorified in the Son. If you ask Me anything in My name, I will do it"* (John 14:13-14). The expression is awkward. We don't usually request something from someone in his/her own name. In fact, some manuscripts leave out the "me" (με) and insert "the Father" (τὸν πατέρα) in its place. There is, however, strong external manuscript evidence for "me" being the original text and the internal evidence is compelling as well. It seems more likely that a scribe copying the text by hand would make the mistake of omitting "me" and supplying "the Father" to avoid the awkwardness of the sentence. So the best reading is με not τὸν πατέρα.

We can ask Jesus in Jesus' name to answer our requests. Further support for praying directly to Jesus comes from the pronouns in both verses. Jesus says in verse 13, *"Whatever you ask ... I (ἐγὼ) will do."* He makes the "I" emphatic in verse 14. *"If you ask Me ... I will do it"* (ἐγὼ ποιήσω). The ἐγὼ reinforces the με and Jesus will do (ποιήσω) what we ask Him to do.

Jesus makes an extraordinary promise to answer our requests whether we ask the Father (vs. 13) or Jesus directly (vs. 14). The natural implication of verse 13 is that we ask the Father. The explicit teaching of verse 14 is that we ask Jesus. Whether we ask the Father or we ask the Son, we are to ask "in Jesus name." Whether we ask the Father or we ask the Son, Jesus answers the prayer request. Whatever we ask, Jesus will do! He carries out the answers to our prayers.

The Father is in the Son. The Son is in the Father (vs. 10-11). To pray to one is to pray to the other. We pray to either Father or Son in Jesus name. Prayer is not a magic formula that unlocks the power of God to fulfill our wants. Prayer is "love-talk" - the whispers of intimate conversation. Our requests that Jesus promises to answer reflect that intimacy. Prayer flows out of our intimate union with both Father and Son. Answers to our prayers flow out of the intimate union of the Father with the Son. Their intimacy with each other in purpose grounds our intimacy with them in prayer.

John 14:15-17

If you love me,
15 Ἐὰν ἀγαπᾶτέ με,
    You will obey my orders
    τὰς ἐντολὰς τὰς ἐμὰς τηρήσετε·

and I will ask the Father
16 κἀγὼ ἐρωτήσω τὸν πατέρα

    And He will give another legal friend to you,
    καὶ ἄλλον παράκλητον δώσει ὑμῖν,
        in order that with you forever He might be,
        ἵνα μεθ' ὑμῶν εἰς τὸν αἰῶνα ᾖ,

    The Spirit of truth
17 τὸ πνεῦμα τῆς ἀληθείας,
    Whom the world is not able to accept,
    ὃ ὁ κόσμος οὐ δύναται λαβεῖν,
        because it does neither perceives Him nor knows (Him)
        ὅτι οὐ θεωρεῖ αὐτὸ οὐδὲ γινώσκει·
        You, yourselves, know Him,
        ὑμεῖς γινώσκετε αὐτό,
            because with you He remains and in you, He will be.
            ὅτι παρ' ὑμῖν μένει καὶ ἐν ὑμῖν ἔσται.

JOHN 14

PREACHING POINTS

There are two main preaching points centered around loving obedience and the promised Spirit from the Father. The second preaching points carries two subpoints teaching us more about the role of the Spirit in our lives and in this world. The central idea should tie the two main preaching points together.

Central Idea:

1. (v.15)

2. (vs.16-17)

Briefly, identify two contemporary life parallels to these verses.

CLP #1

CLP #2

LOVE'S OBEDIENCE

Freedom in our obedience flows out of the fullness of our love. Jesus said, *"If you love Me, you will keep My commandments"* (John 14:15). Obedience is the natural, but not obligatory, consequence of love. Love does not demand obedience, but obedience expresses love.

The verse is conditional. It is a third class condition sometimes called a "more probable future condition" (DM, p.290). The construction suggests an element of uncertainty expressed in the future tense of the apodosis - *"you will keep my commands."* The majority text uses an imperative (τηρήσατε), but the better attested reading is a future indicative (τηρήσετε) which also fits better with the third class condition and the future tense of "ask" (ἐρωτήσω) in verse 16.

The stress of the apodosis is on "my" commands. The pronoun is emphatic (τὰς ἐμὰς). There is absolute authority bound up in this pronoun. Moses told the Israelites, *"These are the things the Lord has commanded you"* (Exodus 35:1). Now Jesus talks about *"my commandments"* recalling the Lord's commands in the Law of God. Instead of making obedience a response to authority, Jesus teaches an obedience that flows from love. Here is no legalistic duty to obey but a free desire to obey with an element of uncertainty in the obedience because Jesus seeks the heart more than the act of obedience.

How then can we learn to love Jesus more? We can learn to love Jesus more as we study the words and the will of the one we love. Jesus promises us help for our obedience as we learn His ways. Verse 16 is tied grammatically to verse 15. The promised "helper" will be in us helping us as we obey out of a heart of love.

Intimacy with Jesus is the foundation for obedience to His will.

ANOTHER HELPER

Our intimacy with Jesus is grounded in the intimacy of the Trinity. We catch a glimpse of this spiritual intimacy in John 14:16 where Jesus promises us, *"I will ask the Father, and He will give you another Helper."* The Father's gift of a Helper for us comes at the request of the Son on our behalf. Jesus' request to the Father rises from an intimate conversation about us with the Father.

The verb translated *"will ask"* (ἐρωτήσω) suggests an open dialogue between two people face to face. It meant to ask a question in a conversation. Another common word for "ask" (αἰτέω) is used of making a request from an inferior to a superior. When the disciples ask God for anything in prayer, αἰτέω is used (see John 14:14), but αἰτέω is never used of Jesus' own requests to God. The word for Jesus' requests to the Father is either ἐρωτάω or δέομαι. The word ἐρωτάω indicates an intimate conversational setting (NIDNTT, 3: 856-857).

Jesus promises the disciples that in the near future (note future tense) He will have an intimate conversation with the Father. The topic of this conversation will be us! I take it that Jesus continues to have intimate conversations with the Father about us. The result of these intimate conversations is that we continue to enjoy the help we need with the problems we face in this life.

Jesus asks the Father to give us another (ἄλλον) Helper. The word "another" (ἄλλον) indicates another helper who is different but not antithetical to the first helper. The new helper is an additional helper. There are two Greek words for "another." The first word for "another" (ἕτερος) tends to distinguish two subjects. The second word for "another" (ἄλλος) tends to add two subjects although the meanings often merge. The second word is the word used here. Jesus requests more help, or additional help, for us.

Jesus, of course, is the first Helper. He has just pledged His help in verses 13-14. What we ask in His name, He pledges to do for us as long as it brings glory to the Father. Jesus is still our advocate or helper today. *"And if anyone sins, we have an Advocate (Helper - same word) with the Father, Jesus Christ the righteous"* (1 John 2:1). As if Jesus is not enough help for us, Jesus requests an additional helper. We are doubly helped by the Son and the Spirit as a gift from our Father rising out of His ongoing intimate conversations with the Son about us.

Thank you, Father, for your loving gift!
Thank you, Jesus, for your loving request!
Thank you, Spirit, for your loving help!

WHAT IS A PARACLETE?

Jesus promised us an additional Paraclete from the Father (John 14:16, 26) - one who would be like Him. A quick survey of translations finds the following meanings for Paraclete (παράκλητον): comforter (KJV), advocate (NIV), helper (ESV & NASB), and counselor (RSV). The word Paraclete is so rich in meaning that it is probably impossible to find a single English word which can plumb its depths (MOR, p. 666).

The verb form of this word (παρακαλέω) means "to call along side" and can be used for either exhortation or consolation (BAGD). The noun (παράκλητος) can certainly carry a sense of comfort or consolation, and the early church fathers translated it this way. The word can also be used in a technical sense of attorney or advocate. We can see this sense of the word used for Jesus and His role in God's courtroom when we sin. *"If anyone sins, we have an Advocate (παράκλητον) with the Father, Jesus Christ, the righteous"* (1 John 2:1). Jesus is our defense attorney whenever we are charged with sin before a Holy God. The Holy Spirit, in John 14:16, is "another" παράκλητον like Jesus so many opt for "advocate" in keeping with the image of a defense attorney in 1 John 2:1.

However, by the time of the New Testament, the technical legal meaning of the word had diminished in usage (BAGD), and the word had taken on a more general meaning of a helper - one who comes to the aid of another. This is a common way to understand the word. The context of John 14 supports a meaning that is less technical and more supportive given the emphasis on teaching and peace (John 14:26-27). Helper moves us in this direction, but I think it loses some of the richness of the meaning we find for Paraclete.

The word Paraclete was used for a friend of an accused person, not his hired attorney. The friend was more than just a helper. He was called alongside to speak about a person's character and provide personal support for his friend in need (MM, p.485). He was first a friend. He was a "pleader" on behalf of his friend. I like the thought that the Holy Spirit, as our Paraclete, is a "legal friend" (MOR, p.649). He is our helper in a legal sense, but he is more than a hired helper and more than a legal advocate. The Paraclete is a true friend who pleads for us and stands with us in our times of need.

We have two friends in high places. Jesus is our first Paraclete. He is now in heaven. The Holy Spirit is our friend on earth. He is with us, and in us, here and now. They both vouch for us when we have needs so that we find peace in their friendship. We have two friends who stand with us through our struggles in life - one friend in heaven and one friend on earth! With friends like these, we are never alone and never at a loss.

THE FRIENDSHIP OF THE SPIRIT

The role of the Holy Spirit in the lives of believers changed significantly with the physical departure of Jesus from this world. Jesus promised His disciples that the Father "will give" (δώσει) the disciples a friend to come alongside them when He is gone (14:16). This friend is called the "Spirit of Truth" (14:17) and the "Holy Spirit" (14:26). He is a friend who provides a depth of intimacy we could never have enjoyed prior to the departure of Jesus.

Jesus told His disciples that they currently knew this friend *"because He abides with you and will be in you"* (14:17). The external textual support is strong for either a present tense or a future tense, but the context requires a future tense. There would be no reason for Jesus to request another "friend" if the friend was already there in the same way as He will be there later. The future tense of "will give" (δώσει) in verse 16 and the undisputed future tenses in verse 26 require us to understand the coming of the Spirit as future to that day. We enjoy a more intimate work of the Holy Spirit than believers in the Old Testament experienced.

Three prepositions teach us about the changing role of the Spirit. In verse 16, Jesus says that the friend "may be with you forever" (μεθ'). In verse 17, the Spirit "is abiding with" them (παρ'). A change is coming, and the Spirit "will be in" them (ἐν). We cannot make ironclad distinctions between prepositions, but, when used in a context like this, we can draw out some nuances of meaning in the contrasting phrases.

The base meaning of the preposition μετά is "in the midst of" or with someone in the sense of a union or association (ATR, p.609). The fellowship of the Spirit is with us in our Christian lives (2 Cor. 13:14). The simplest meaning of the second preposition παρά means beside or alongside of someone. It emphasizes His personal presence with us. Jesus has already been with them in this sense along with the Holy Spirit (14:25), and Jesus promises to continue to be with them in the future (14:23). The idea is that both are with us in the sense of at our homes (ATR, p.614).

The third preposition ἐν introduces the new role of the Spirit. The emphasis of ἐν in this context is that our friend will not just be near us but inside of us. This is the basic meaning (ATR, p. 586), and Jesus implies this very distinction here regarding the changing role of the Spirit. The Spirit had formerly been alongside them but now will be inside them. This will be the new role of the Spirit unknown and not experienced before this time.

The third preposition ἐν is the most intimate of the three. This preposition is a favorite word used by Jesus to explain our new intimacy with God in this chapter, so we should understand it in its full force. Jesus has just told them in verse 9 that He has been with them (μετά), so they should have known the Father because Jesus is in (ἐν) the Father and the Father is in (ἐν) Jesus (14:11). He tells us to ask our requests in (ἐν) His name (14:13-14). Jesus culminates the lesson in intimacy in verse 20 by saying, *"I am in (ἐν) the Father, and you are in (ἐν) Me, and I am in (ἐν) you"* (14:20).

The Trinity is our foundation for intimacy. We can enjoy a deeper intimacy with God because our friend, the Holy Spirit, lives inside us. We enjoy the intimacy of our friend named Jesus who lives in perfect intimacy with the Father. We are wrapped in an intimate embrace with the Godhead because our hearts are joined as one with all three persons of the Godhead. It is a friendship deeper than any words and stronger than the strongest bonds.

John 14:18-21

I will not leave you behind without parents,
18 Οὐκ ἀφήσω ὑμᾶς ὀρφανούς,
    I am coming to you.
    ἔρχομαι πρὸς ὑμᾶς.

        Still, a little while and the world no longer sees me,
        19 ἔτι μικρὸν καὶ ὁ κόσμος με οὐκέτι θεωρεῖ,
But you, yourselves, (will) see me,
ὑμεῖς δὲ θεωρεῖτέ με,
        because I, myself, am alive
        ὅτι ἐγὼ ζῶ
        You, yourselves, also will be alive.
        καὶ ὑμεῖς ζήσετε.
    In that day you, yourselves, will comprehend
    20 ἐν ἐκείνῃ τῇ ἡμέρᾳ γνώσεσθε ὑμεῖς
        that I (am) in my Father
        ὅτι ἐγὼ ἐν τῷ πατρί μου
        and you (are) in me
        καὶ ὑμεῖς ἐν ἐμοὶ
        and I (am) in you.
        κἀγὼ ἐν ὑμῖν.

The one who has my orders
21 ὁ ἔχων τὰς ἐντολάς μου
And obeys them
καὶ τηρῶν αὐτὰς
    that one is the one who loves me
    ἐκεῖνός ἐστιν ὁ ἀγαπῶν με·
        and the one who loves me will be loved
        ὁ δὲ ἀγαπῶν με ἀγαπηθήσεται
            by my Father
            ὑπὸ τοῦ πατρός μου,
        and I will love him
        κἀγὼ ἀγαπήσω αὐτὸν
        and I will disclose myself to him.
        καὶ ἐμφανίσω αὐτῷ ἐμαυτόν.

JOHN 14

PREACHING POINTS

The main preaching point is Jesus' promise not to abandon them as helpless, without support. This would be the central idea of the passage. He is coming to them and explains His promise with two subordinate preaching points. First, comes His promise that they will understand true spiritual life in that day. Second, their loving obedience to Him is the condition for His full disclosure to them.

Central Idea: (v.18)

1. (vs.19-20)

2. (v.21)

Briefly, identify two contemporary life parallels to these verses.

CLP #1

CLP #2

LIFE IN LIFE

Jesus promised His disciples that He would not abandon them as orphans but would come back to them after the resurrection (John 14:18-19; 16:16-22). "In that day" (ἐν ἐκείνῃ τῇ ἡμέρᾳ) after the resurrection, they would experience a mutual indwelling with the triune God (John 14:20). Jesus must be referring to the period from the resurrection to the ascension. He has just promised them the indwelling of the Spirit (John 14:17), and, after the resurrection, Jesus breathed the Spirit on them (John 20:20-23) as a temporary infilling until the Day of Pentecost following His ascension to heaven.

Our deepest intimacy with God comes from this mutual indwelling. Jesus said, *"In that day you will know that I am in the Father, and you in ME, and I in you"* (John 14:20). The triple repetition of the preposition "in" (ἐν) indicates "the space within which something is found" (BAGD, p. 258). Jesus is in the Father. This is the foundational indwelling for our benefit. We are in Jesus, and Jesus is in us. The Son and the Spirit are in us who are in the Son who is in the Father. It is a position of amazing security like our most precious documents placed inside a fire box that is, in turn, placed inside a bank vault!

It is also a position of deepest, life-giving, life-sustaining intimacy. Jesus is in us, and we are in Jesus like a fish is in water, and water is the fish; or like a bird is in the air, and the air is in the bird (SLJ). This total and mutual immersion of life in life forms a spiritual connection deeper than the most intimate human bond can ever hope to achieve.

Here, in this verse, we find the basis for the extended metaphor of the "Vine and Branches" (John 15). Jesus explains our deep connection with Him in the analogy of the vine and branches. A cleft graft uniting a fruit-bearing shoot with the stock of a vine is literally a linkage of life inside life. The stock is split, and the branch is sliced so that the branch fits deep into - and matches up with - the stock. The life of the stock flows into the branch.

We are in Jesus, and Jesus is in us - life in life. His life flows in us who are living in Him.

FULL DISCLOSURE

How can we know Jesus? We can know Jesus only to the extent that He discloses Himself to us just like in any intimate relationship. Intimacy requires self-disclosure, and self-disclosure only takes place in the context of a committed and trustworthy love. Apart from a commitment to love, there will be limited self-disclosure, so the depth of a friendship depends on love's commitment.

"He who has My commandments and keeps them is the one who loves Me; and he who loves Me will be loved by My Father, and I will love him and will disclose Myself to him" (John 14:21).

Obedience to Jesus is the evidence of our love for Jesus. It is not enough to have (ἔχων) His commands. We must keep (τηρῶν) them. The "having" and the "keeping" are ongoing actions that prove an ongoing love (ἀγαπῶν). My friendship with Jesus does not depend on what others think about me or how successful I am in ministry. My identity does not come from my ministry. My identity comes from my identification with Him. The level of intimacy I enjoy with Jesus depends on my obedience to Him as the proof of my love for Him.

Jesus promises to disclose Himself to those who love Him as demonstrated by our obedience to Him. The word "disclose" (ἐμφανίσω) is in the future tense. Jesus promised to disclose Himself to the disciples in a way that He had not yet disclosed Himself to them, although serving together for the past three years on earth. The word means to "reveal" and emphasizes a self-revealing or self-disclosure. It was a word used in the Greek translation of Exodus 33:13 in the context of a theophany - a self-revelation of God. Jesus promised full disclosure of Himself but only to those who love Him.

Jude was shocked (John 14:22). He expected a visible and public revelation of Jesus as God. He could not grasp a self-disclosure that was personal, private and intimate. How could Jesus reveal Himself to those who loved and obeyed Him in a way that He did not reveal Himself to the world? Isn't full messianic disclosure public? This was Jude's expectation. He did not grasp the point Jesus was making about the intimacy of true friendship and the self-disclosure that takes place between friends.

The self-disclosure Jesus promised was a spiritual, personal and private illumination in the heart of a true disciple. Jesus said, *"I will disclose Myself to HIM."* The word was used figuratively in the Jewish wisdom literature of something that took place in the soul of a person (BAGD, p.257; BERN, p.550). Jesus promised to disclose Himself to those who love Him in the intimacy of a friendship. This is the language of the Spirit with our spirits (John 14:26; 16:14-15). It is relational language. The greater our love for Jesus, the more He discloses Himself to us and the deeper our friendship grows.

John 14:22-24

    Judas, not Iscariot, said to him
22 Λέγει αὐτῷ Ἰούδας, οὐχ ὁ Ἰσκαριώτης·
        Lord, what has happened
        κύριε, [καὶ] τί γέγονεν
            that to us you are going to disclose yourself
            ὅτι ἡμῖν μέλλεις ἐμφανίζειν σεαυτὸν
                and not to the world?
                καὶ οὐχὶ τῷ κόσμῳ;
    Jesus answered and said to him
23 ἀπεκρίθη Ἰησοῦς καὶ εἶπεν αὐτῷ·

If anyone loves me he will obey my word
ἐάν τις ἀγαπᾷ με τὸν λόγον μου τηρήσει,
    and my Father will love him
    καὶ ὁ πατήρ μου ἀγαπήσει αὐτὸν
    and to him, we will come
    καὶ πρὸς αὐτὸν ἐλευσόμεθα
    and a home with him we will make.
    καὶ μονὴν παρ' αὐτῷ ποιησόμεθα.

The one who is not loving me does not obey my words
24 ὁ μὴ ἀγαπῶν με τοὺς λόγους μου οὐ τηρεῖ·
    and the word that you are hearing is not mine
    καὶ ὁ λόγος ὃν ἀκούετε οὐκ ἔστιν ἐμὸς
        but (the word of) the Father who sent me.
        ἀλλὰ τοῦ πέμψαντός με πατρός.

JOHN 14

PREACHING POINTS

The opening dialogue between Judas' question and Jesus' reply sets the stage for the two main preaching points. Obedience demonstrates love and disobedience proves a lack of love. The result of loving obedience is greater intimacy with God, but the result of disobedience is a broken relationship with God by God's decree. The central idea should summarize these two thoughts.

Central Idea:

1. (v.23)

2. (v.24)

Briefly identify two contemporary life parallels to these verses.

CLP #1

CLP #2

LIMITED SELF-DISCLOSURE

Jesus has just said that the world will no longer see Him, but His disciples will see Him because they love Him (Jn. 14:19-21). He says to the one who loves Him, *"I will love Him and will disclose* (ἐμφανίσω) *Myself to him* (14:21). Love is the condition for self-disclosure.

Jesus' statement precipitated Judas' question. *"Lord, what then has happened that You are going to disclose* (ἐμφανίζειν) *Yourself to us and not to the world?"* There is a textual problem in the opening words of the question. "Lord" (Κύριε) is followed by "and" (καὶ) in brackets indicating a disputed word in the text. The external evidence for the omission of καὶ is stronger than the evidence for inclusion. "Lord" (Κύριε) was a sacred name that was often abbreviated to κε and pronounced like καὶ leading to copyists adding καὶ to the text (METZ, p.245).

Judas was confused. He thought of Christ's self-disclosure in physical terms as a visible, bodily revelation (MEY, 3:420). How could such a disclosure be limited to those who love Jesus? The verb (ἐμφανίζω) means to show or make visible. The word comes from the root φαίνω meaning to shine like the sun. The dead came out of their tombs (Mt. 27:53) and were made visible (ἐνεφανίσθησαν) to many. Peter later says (Acts 10:40) that God raised Jesus from the dead and "He became visible" (ἐμφανῆ). The author of Hebrews (Heb. 9:24) tells us that Jesus entered heaven "to appear" (ἐμφανισθῆναι) before the face of God on our behalf (TDNT, 9:7).

How, then, can Jesus be visible to us and not to the world? We, too, ask Judas' question. Jesus clearly speaks of self-disclosure as being more than physical visibility. This understanding does not deny the truth of a bodily resurrection, but Jesus takes His self-disclosure to a deeper level. His self-disclosure to His followers is different than His self-disclosure to the world because His self-disclosure pulls back the curtain that hides the secrets of His inner nature. Jesus chooses to reveal the depths of His spiritual, emotional and mental thoughts only to those who love Him.

Our spiritual intimacy with Jesus depends on His self-disclosure to us.

CLOSENESS WITH JESUS

Our love for Jesus demonstrated in our obedience to Him is the condition for closeness with Him (Jn. 14:23). Jesus says, *"If anyone loves Me, he will keep My word."* The condition (ἐάν) with the subjunctive "loves" (ἀγαπᾷ) looks to the future with an element of uncertainty but implied probability (DM, p.290). Jesus promises closeness assuming the fulfillment of the condition.

Jesus says, *"We will come* (ἐλευσόμεθα) *to Him."* The verb combined with the preposition "to" (πρὸς) indicates movement (MOU, p.52). The prepositional phrase "to Him" (πρὸς αὐτὸν) is in an emphatic position in the sentence. God (Father and Son) come to us. We do not go to them! We love and obey. God promises to come to us. Jesus says that he stands knocking at the door of our hearts (Rev. 3:20). If we listen to His voice and open the door, Jesus says, "I will come into" (εἰσελεύσομαι) – an intensive form of the same root (ἔρχομαι).

Jesus continues. *"We will make (ποιησόμεθα) a room (μονὴν) with (παρ') him."* The verb (ποιέω) means to create. It refers to actions someone takes to bring about or accomplish an event or state of being including a dinner or banquet (BAGD, p.681). God brings about a room that He shares with us. The word translated "room" (μονὴν) comes from the verb to remain (μένω) and occurs only twice in the Gospel of John (TDNT, 4:580). The other place is John 14:2 where Jesus promises dwelling places in His Father's house. The word can mean a "night stop" or "resting place" like an inn where a traveler stays (BRO, p.618), but it seems better to mean a permanent resting place or home in view of the root meaning to remain (NIDNTT, 3:229; TDNT, 4:580).

God comes to us and creates a home with (παρ') us. The preposition (παρά) with the dative case indicates "rest with" or rest in "the presence of" another (MOU, p.52). Jesus chooses to abide with us as we love and obey Jesus. He sets the stage with these words for the teaching of the vine and the branches in John 15. Jesus commands us to remain in Him (Jn. 15:4). The verbal root (μένω) is used to emphasize our abiding in Him. He promises to make His home with us both now (Jn. 14:23) and in heaven (Jn. 14:2).

Lord, stay close to me as I rest in you. Don't let me do anything to drive you from the home you have made with me and the friendship we enjoy.

John 14:25-27

These things I have said to you
25 Ταῦτα λελάληκα ὑμῖν
    while remaining with you
    παρ' ὑμῖν μένων·
But the legal friend,
26 * ὁ δὲ παράκλητος,
    The Holy Spirit
    τὸ πνεῦμα τὸ ἅγιον,
        whom the Father will send in my name,
        ὃ πέμψει ὁ πατὴρ ἐν τῷ ὀνόματί μου,
    He will teach you all things
    ἐκεῖνος ὑμᾶς διδάξει πάντα
    and He will remind you (of) all things
    καὶ ὑπομνήσει ὑμᾶς πάντα
        which I said to you.
        ἃ εἶπον ὑμῖν [ἐγώ].

Peace I leave behind with you,
27 Εἰρήνην ἀφίημι ὑμῖν,
    My peace I am giving to you
    εἰρήνην τὴν ἐμὴν δίδωμι ὑμῖν·
        not as the world gives
        οὐ καθὼς ὁ κόσμος δίδωσιν
            I, myself am giving to you.
            ἐγὼ δίδωμι ὑμῖν.

Do not allow your heart to be stirred up
μὴ ταρασσέσθω ὑμῶν ἡ καρδία
    neither let it be cowardly.
    μηδὲ δειλιάτω.

JOHN 14

PREACHING POINTS

The central idea of the passage comes in the conclusion. Jesus' twin commands against being upset or fearful constitute the main point of the teaching. The two supporting preaching points tell us the resources He gives to us to fight our fears. He gives us His friend and His peace.

Central Idea: (v.27b)

1. (v.26)

2. (v.27a)

Briefly, identify two contemporary life parallels to these verses.

CLP #1

CLP #2

MY PEACE!

"Peace, I leave with you; My peace I give to you; not as the world gives do I give to you. Do not let your heart be troubled, not let it be fearful" (John 14:27).

We, humans, perceive peace as the absence of conflict, chaos, and disorder. Jesus presents peace as the presence of harmony, wholeness, and order. Biblical peace is not the absence of negative emotions. Christ's peace is the presence of personal convictions leading to a sense of well-being. Peace (εἰρήνην) reflects the Old Testament teaching of "shalom." Biblical peace is an assurance of order in the midst of disorder, wholeness in the midst of chaos, and well-being in the midst of conflict because we know all matters are in our Father's hands.

Jesus leaves us peace and gives us His peace. The two verbs help us understand the peace we have in life. First, Jesus leaves (ἀφίημι) peace to us. The word is often translated "forgive" or "pardon" and can even mean "divorce" in the sense of sending someone away. Here, however, Jesus uses the word in its most common sense of leaving behind something in the manner of a bequest to a loved one. The same word was used in John 14:18 where Jesus said, *"I will not leave you as orphans."* The bequest of Jesus is peace, not abandonment. Jesus leaves behind a sense of inner wholeness and order despite outer chaos and conflict.

Second, Jesus gives (δίδωμι) us His peace. Peace is a gift or a bestowal in the midst of our personal experiences. Jesus leaves us with a sense of order in life because He is in control, but He also gives us a sense of well-being that we can experience in the middle of our circumstances. We will be alright in the end because He controls the end! Three times He uses the verb to give (δίδωμι). Jesus tells us *"I, myself (ἐγώ), give you My (ἐμὴν) peace.* Wholeness in the midst of chaos, order in the midst of disorder, and harmony in the midst of conflict are His personal gifts to us. His peace is not like the peace of this world. The peace of the world is dependent on circumstances - actually, the absence of bad circumstances. The peace Jesus gives is our inner wholeness to transcend our circumstances.

Life is filled with troubles and fears, but we don't have to succumb to either troubles or fears. The verb "to be troubled" (ταρασσέσθω) means to be stirred up, unsettled or thrown into confusion (cf. John 14:1), but we don't have to be unsettled or stirred up because our trust is in Jesus. The verb for "fearful" (δειλιάτω.) means to be cowardly or timid. Jesus commands us not to be confused or cowardly because He gives us inner assurance that everything is under His control.

We can face any situation with His peace.

John 14:28-31

You have heard that I said to you
28 ἠκούσατε ὅτι ἐγὼ εἶπον ὑμῖν·
    I am going away, and I am coming to you
    ὑπάγω καὶ ἔρχομαι πρὸς ὑμᾶς.
        If you loved me, you would have been glad
        εἰ ἠγαπᾶτέ με ἐχάρητε ἂν
            that I am going to the Father,
            ὅτι πορεύομαι πρὸς τὸν πατέρα,
                because the Father is greater than me.
                ὅτι ὁ πατὴρ μείζων μού ἐστιν.
    And now I have told you before it happens,
    29 καὶ νῦν εἴρηκα ὑμῖν πρὶν γενέσθαι,
        in order that when it does happen, you may believe
        ἵνα ὅταν γένηται πιστεύσητε.

I will no longer talk much with you,
30 οὐκέτι πολλὰ λαλήσω μεθ' ὑμῶν,
    for the ruler of the world, arrives
    ἔρχεται γὰρ ὁ τοῦ κόσμου ἄρχων·
        and in me, he has nothing,
        καὶ ἐν ἐμοὶ οὐκ ἔχει οὐδέν,
    but in order that the world might know
    31 ἀλλ' ἵνα γνῷ ὁ κόσμος
        that I love the Father,
        ὅτι ἀγαπῶ τὸν πατέρα,
            as also the Father ordered me,
            καὶ καθὼς ἐνετείλατό μοι ὁ πατήρ,
                so I do.
                οὕτως ποιῶ.
    Get up, let us go away from here.
    ἐγείρεσθε, ἄγωμεν ἐντεῦθεν.

JOHN 14

PREACHING POINTS

The two main preaching points revolve around why Jesus predicted His departure and why He will no longer be talking to them. First Jesus explains why it is so important that He prepare them for going away. Second Jesus explains why He must go away. He faces the devil out of obedience to the Father. The central idea should summarize the two main preaching points.

Central Idea:

1. (vs.28-29)

2. (vs.30-31)

Briefly, identify two contemporary life parallels to these verses.

CLP #1

CLP #2

THE JOY OF TRUE LOVE

Love's deep joy comes from love's self-sacrifice. When I truly love someone, I experience joy in sacrificing myself for that one. The principle is counter-intuitive to our human expectations. Jesus demonstrated the principle on the cross and taught it to us in John 14:28.

"You heard that I said to you, 'I go away, and I will come to you.' If you loved Me, you would have rejoiced because I go to the Father, for the Father is greater than I."

The disciples were saddened by their coming loss. Their myopic self-interest interfered with Christ's eternal interests making their sadness selfish. The conditional sentence is a second class condition where the condition is assumed to be unfulfilled or contrary to fact (ATR, p. 1012). The protasis is "if you loved Me" (εἰ ἠγαπᾶτέ με). The imperfect tense indicates they were not loving Him on an ongoing basis. Jesus does not doubt that they have loved Him, but their sadness at His going proves they were not continuing to love Him. If they had kept on loving Him, they would have experienced joy even in His departure (ATR, p. 1015).

The apodosis - *"you would have rejoiced"* at My going - (ἐχάρητε ἄν) - acknowledges the reality of their joylessness. The verb means to experience gladness. They were "losing" Jesus, and their sense of loss led to sadness because they could not see beyond their self-interest. Their sadness was rooted in their limited self-interest. They could not see that letting Jesus go would lead to greater joy. Some suggest that Jesus was demonstrating a playfully tender appeal for their love (BERN, 2:555). I see it more as a wistful appeal. Jesus wished they could love Him so much they would rejoice in His departure because what He was doing for them was so much better than they could possibly guess.

In reality, our true self-interest lies in seeking Christ's greater interests where we experience real joy. Jesus longs for us to love Him so deeply that we can rejoice in Him even in our losses. The deepest love rejoices in the greatest loss by looking beyond our loss to see His love. The depth of my love for Him is measured by the joy I feel in His love even in my loss.

THE CROSS AND THE RULER

Jesus tells the disciples that He will not speak much more with them because *"the ruler of the world is coming"* (John 14:30). The ruler is Satan, and the coming is his coming to kill Jesus. Satan choreographs the events leading to the cross. The Pharisees, Pontius Pilate, and the crowds are secondary causes of the cross. The first cause is Satan. The cross is a cosmic battle fought by Satan against God through human proxies who are dominated by their ruler.

Only one man in the history of the world had no foothold that Satan could use to rule him - Jesus! Jesus said, *"he has nothing in Me"* (John 14:30). The *"in Me"* (ἐν ἐμοὶ) is placed first in the clause for emphasis. The double negative added further intensity to Jesus' affirmation (οὐκ ἔχει οὐδέν). Literally Jesus says, *"in Me not he has nothing."* The clause is translated idiomatically in several ways. *"He has no claim on Me"* (ESV). *"He has no hold over Me"* (NIV). The ruler of this world could find nothing in Jesus that he could use to rule Jesus in any way.

Satan rules this world by finding flaws he can use to dominate people. We are all flawed by sin and Satan uses these sinful flaws to rule us. There were no spiritual weaknesses or sinful flaws in Jesus. Pontius Pilate used a similar expression to announce that he could find no guilt (οὐδεμίαν ... αἰτίαν) in Him (ἐν αὐτῷ) (John 18:38). Jesus was sinless as the author of Hebrews later writes (Heb. 4:15), but His sinlessness is more than merely a lack of sinful actions or behaviors. Jesus claims here that His sinlessness is a "necessary causal condition" (MEY, p. 424) for His freedom from the power of the ruler of this world. The sinless perfection of Jesus was intrinsic to His nature giving Satan no foothold in His life.

The sinless perfection of Jesus in His very nature is the necessary foundation for His substitutionary sacrifice on the cross. Satan could seize nothing in Jesus to rule so Jesus could offer Himself as a sacrifice of love on the cross thereby defeating the one who had choreographed the crucifixion. Jesus freely gave Himself to show the world that He loved and obeyed the Father as He says in the next verse (John 14:31). The first motivating focus of Jesus on the cross was love for His Father. We take second place in the mind of Jesus. The cross was a free offering of love satisfying the Father on our behalf, precisely because Satan had no foothold in Jesus that he could use to defeat God's plan to save humanity from the ruler of this world.

JOHN 15

John 15:1-4

I, myself, am the authentic vine and my Father is the gardener.
Ἐγώ εἰμι ἡ ἄμπελος ἡ ἀληθινὴ καὶ ὁ πατὴρ μου ὁ γεωργός ἐστιν.
    Every branch
    2 πᾶν κλῆμα
            in me
            ἐν ἐμοὶ
            not bearing fruit
            μὴ φέρον καρπὸν
    he lifts it up,
    αἴρει αὐτό,
and every branch bearing fruit
καὶ πᾶν τὸ καρπὸν φέρον
    He cleanses it
    καθαίρει αὐτὸ
        in order that it might bear much fruit
        ἵνα καρπὸν πλείονα φέρῃ.
    Already you, yourselves, are clean
    3 ἤδη ὑμεῖς καθαροί ἐστε
        On account of the word which I have spoken to you,
        διὰ τὸν λόγον ὃν λελάληκα ὑμῖν·

Remain in me, and I in you.
4 μείνατε ἐν ἐμοί, κἀγὼ ἐν ὑμῖν.
    Just as the branch is not able to bear fruit by itself
    καθὼς τὸ κλῆμα οὐ δύναται καρπὸν φέρειν ἀφ' ἑαυτοῦ
        except it remains in the vine,
        ἐὰν μὴ μένῃ ἐν τῇ ἀμπέλῳ,
so neither you
οὕτως οὐδὲ ὑμεῖς
    except you remain in me.
    ἐὰν μὴ ἐν ἐμοὶ μένητε.

JOHN 15

PREACHING POINTS

There are two main preaching points in these verses. The first is a statement and the second a command based on the statement. The statement introduces an explanation of the process God uses to produce fruit in us. Notice the play on words between "cleanse" (καθαίρει) and "clean" (καθαροί) in verse 3 which helps explain the second stage of the process. The command tells us what we need to do to free Him to produce fruit in us. The central idea should summarize these two main points.

Central Idea:

1. (vs.1-3)

2. (v.4)

Briefly, identify two contemporary life parallels to these verses.

CLP #1

CLP #2

FRUITLESS CHRISTIANS

The extended metaphor of the vine and the branches in John 15 deals with fruit bearing through abiding in Christ. The word "fruit" (καρπός) is used eight times in verses 1-16. The word "abide" (μένω) is used 11 times in verses 1-16. To "abide" means to remain or continue. Branches produce fruit by remaining connected to the vine. The life flowing from Jesus (the Vine) produces the fruit in believers (the branches.).

Jesus is speaking about real believers. The Father is the gardener. Jesus is the vine and believers are the branches. Jesus says that the gardener will take action regarding *"every branch in Me that does not bear fruit"* (John 15:2). The branches, Jesus says, are "in Me" (ἐν ἐμοί). A branch is not a branch if it is not "in Me," Jesus says. He is speaking only about branches that are in union with Jesus. Every branch in the metaphor is connected to Christ. Jesus is not talking about branches from other vines. These branches are all from His vine. Therefore, all branches in this metaphor are genuine believers.

Some branches, Jesus implies, are not bearing fruit (μὴ φέρον καρπὸν). Bearing (φέρον) is an attributive participle describing fruit (καρπὸν). An attributive participle is used to attribute a characteristic or an action to the noun it modifies (BD, p.212). The resulting clause explains the branch. The branch Jesus is talking about is a "not bearing fruit" branch. Since all branches are in Christ, this fruitless branch is a fruitless believer.

The participle "bearing" (φέρον) is a present active participle. The branch is not actively producing fruit, and the branch is not currently producing fruit. The time of the participle is connected to the time of the main verb. The main verb, in this case, is also a present tense verb (αἴρει). Therefore, the time of the the participle is present time. The Christian in view is not presently bearing fruit. Jesus is not considering a person who has never borne fruit. A professing - not genuine - Christian would never have borne any fruit. Jesus is not talking about such a person here. He is talking about a believer who is not currently producing fruit, not an unbeliever who pretended to produce fruit.

There are three conclusions we can draw from this opening clause in the metaphor. 1) All branches (believers) are united with Christ. 2) Jesus intends that every believer will bear fruit. 3) Believers, at times, become fruitless, and that fruitlessness must be addressed by the gardener.

THE GARDENER'S JOB

There are two levels of fruitlessness in the analogy of the vine and the branches (John 15:2). There are "no fruit" branches and "some fruit" branches, but both are still branches (Christians). God, the Father, is the gardener. He intends that all branches will bear "much fruit" so He cultivates the branches in order to make them fruitful. What does the gardener do to make us fruitful Christians?

LEVEL ONE, NO FRUIT CHRISTIANS: *"Every branch in Me that does not bear fruit, He takes away."* The verb translated "takes away" (αἴρει) has three possible meanings (BAGD, p. 24). The first meaning is to lift up or pick up. The verb is used of picking up stones to stone Jesus (John 8:59). The second lexical meaning is to lift up and carry. The man Jesus healed by the pool of Bethesda lifted up and carried his pallet (John 5:8,10,11,12). The third meaning is to take away or remove with the sense of killing someone. The crowds screamed about Jesus to Pilate, *"Away with this man"* (Luke 23:18). So which interpretation would be correct in John 15:2?

Many translations understand the verb in the sense of take away, remove or cut off. This interpretation would be a judgmental action, and verse 6 is used to bolster the argument that this is an act of judgment by God. Some even view it as the "sin unto death" where God removes a person from this life (1 John 5:16). I think it is better to understand the verb in the sense of lift up. This fits better with the sequence of "no fruit" and "some fruit" in this verse. It also conforms to the normal process of gardening. The branches of the vine grow heavy and trail across the ground. If left on the ground, they not only become fruitless but eventually rot. The gardener's first job is to lift up the branches so that they can become fruitful. God does this in our lives whenever we become fruitless because we are mired in the dirt of life. God's first action with fruitless Christians is not to condemn us but to assist us. He lifts us up from the dirtiness of the life into which we have fallen.

LEVEL TWO, SOME FRUIT CHRISTIANS: *"Every branch that bears fruit, He prunes it so that it may bear more fruit."* The verb translated "prune" (καθαίρει) originally meant to clean, sweep or cleanse (NIDNTT, 3:102). The noun form was used as a technical term in agriculture for the use of chemicals to get rid of parasites or fungus. The gardener cleanses the branch of impurities and cuts away the extra woody growths that will hinder the production of fruit. The gardener's goal is to help the branch produce more fruit.

God, the spiritual gardener, takes both of these actions in our lives as needed. When we become mired in the dirt of life and stop producing fruit, God lifts us up so we can grow spiritually. When we are struggling to produce fruit because parasites are affecting our lives or distractions are impeding our growth, the gardener cleanses us with the insecticide of grace and cuts away the distractions in our lives. He will not let us continue as we are but will work to clean us up and prune us down. We may not like the process, but the product is God's luscious fruit.

THE CONDITION FOR BEARING FRUIT

Jesus identifies two conditions - which are really one condition - necessary for fruit bearing in John 15:4. *"Abide in Me, and I in you."* Abiding is necessary for producing fruit. The branch is not capable of producing fruit by itself (ἀφ' ἑαυτοῦ) *"unless it abides in the vine, so neither can you unless you abide in Me."*

Some form of the verb "abide" (μένω) is used 11 times in this chapter. The word means to remain, stay or continue (BAGD, p. 503), and it can have the sense of dwell or live together. For example, the word is used of Mary who stayed or lived with her sister, Elizabeth, for three months (Luke 1:56).

Jesus states the first condition as a command, *"Abide in Me."* It is an aorist active command (μείνατε) indicating action that is undefined in terms of duration. However, the two following uses of abide in this verse are in the present tense indicating that the abiding is to be an ongoing abiding as opposed to an event. We must continue to remain in Christ in order to produce fruit because the power that produces the fruit flows from the vine, Jesus Christ.

The command that we remain in Christ implies that we are already in union with Christ otherwise, how could we remain? Since it is a command for us to take action, it also implies that we can stop remaining in Christ. These two implications, taken together, show us that the verse is talking about our communion with Jesus not our union with Jesus. We are never commanded to be in union with Christ, but we are commanded to stay in communion with Christ. The source of life is being in Him. The source of fruitfulness is remaining in Him.

Jesus states the second condition as an addition to the first, *"And I in you"* (κἀγὼ ἐν ὑμῖν). There are three ways to understand the clause (MOR, p. 670). 1) Jesus is commanding Himself to remain in them, but this makes little sense. 2) The second command is a continuation of the first one. "Remain in Me and make sure I remain in you." 3) The second condition is a promise predicated on the first condition. "Remain in Me, and I promise to remain in you." This makes the best sense of the verse (MEY, p. 430). We can only take care of our part in the relationship. We cannot make Jesus remain in us. He promises to remain in us on the condition that we remain in Him, so the two conditions are one condition. The result of this mutual living together is fruit bearing.

The vine does not block its life flow into the branches, but the branches might block the life flow from the vine. Jesus does not disconnect from us. We disconnect from Him, and the result is fruitlessness. Personal, persistent and continuous intimacy with Jesus produces fruitfulness because He promises that His life will flow into us as we remain connected to Him. Our continuous communion with Jesus unleashes the power of His spiritual life flowing into us to produce fruit.

John 15:5-8

I, myself, am the vine, you are the branches.
5 ἐγώ εἰμι ἡ ἄμπελος, ὑμεῖς τὰ κλήματα.

    The one who remains in me and I in him
    ὁ μένων ἐν ἐμοὶ κἀγὼ ἐν αὐτῷ
        This one bears much fruit,
        οὗτος φέρει καρπὸν πολύν,
            because apart from me you are not able to do anything.
            ὅτι χωρὶς ἐμοῦ οὐ δύνασθε ποιεῖν οὐδέν.
    If anyone does not remain in me,
6 ἐὰν μή τις μένῃ ἐν ἐμοί,
        He is thrown out like a branch
        ἐβλήθη ἔξω ὡς τὸ κλῆμα
        and he is dried up
        καὶ ἐξηράνθη
        and they gather them (neuter to agree with branches)
        καὶ συνάγουσιν αὐτὰ
        and they throw (the branches) into the fire
        καὶ εἰς τὸ πῦρ βάλλουσιν
        and they are burned.
        καὶ καίεται.
    If you remain in me and my words remain in you,
7 ἐὰν μείνητε ἐν ἐμοὶ καὶ τὰ ῥήματά μου ἐν ὑμῖν μείνῃ,
        Ask whatever you want,
        ὃ ἐὰν θέλητε αἰτήσασθε,
            and it will come to be for you
            καὶ γενήσεται ὑμῖν.
    In this, my Father is honored
8 ἐν τούτῳ ἐδοξάσθη ὁ πατήρ μου,
        That you bear much fruit
        ἵνα καρπὸν πολὺν φέρητε
        and you will continue to be my disciples.
        καὶ γένησθε ἐμοὶ μαθηταί.

PREACHING POINTS

The opening sentence of verse 5 governs the paragraph. This sentence is the basis for the central idea. There are four main preaching points in the paragraph. The middle two are conditional sentences about remaining in Christ. The first and the last stress bearing fruit by God's power and for God's glory. Notice that the word for branch is neuter and the relative pronoun is also neuter connecting the gathering to the branches and not people in the metaphor.

Central Idea: (v.5a)

1. (v.5b)

2. (v.6)

3. (v.7)

4. (v.8)

Briefly, identify two contemporary life parallels to these verses.

CLP #1

CLP #2

WHAT HAPPENS TO FRUITLESS CHRISTIANS?

The analogy of the vine and the branches in John 15 is all about fruit bearing. We bear fruit through our communion with Jesus just as the branches bear fruit through their connection to the vine. When we fail to remain in communion with Jesus, we become fruitless because apart from Jesus we can do nothing (John 15:5). Fruitless branches are cast away not because of a lack of life but because of a lack of fruit (John 15:6).

The analogy is an extended figure of speech, and figurative language should not be taken literally. Jesus is not a literal vine and God, the Father, is not a literal gardener. We are not literal branches. The throwing away is not a literal throwing away, and the fire is not a literal fire.

The fruitless believer is thrown away "like a branch" (ὡς τὸ κλῆμα) so what happens to fruitless branches is an illustration of what happens to fruitless Christians. We are judged for our uselessness and set aside as worthless to the master gardener if we become fruitless Christians. There are five verbs that illustrate God's progressive judgment of fruitless Christians.

1) Fruitless Christians are discarded or thrown aside (ἐβλήθη ἔξω). God stops using us in His work. We become useless and hinder His purpose to bear fruit. He sets us aside when we fail to stay in communion with Him. 2) Fruitless Christians are dried up (ἐξηράνθη). The word was used to describe the withering of trees and plants or the drying up of a river (BAGD, p. 548). It is a passive verb. When we are set aside by the gardener (passive voice), the discarding causes us to begin to wither spiritually. We lose our vitality. We become brittle and bitter, and we break easily. Jesus said that if salt loses its potency, it is good for nothing but to be thrown out and trampled (Mt. 5:13). Fruitless Christians may even be removed from life on earth (1 John 5:16).

The next three verbs all have plural subjects. *"They gather them, and they cast them into the fire, and they are burned."* The first two verbs are present active indicatives and the 3rd is a passive, yet all three can be translated as idiomatically passive. All the discussions explaining the identity of "they" in this verse are 'fruitless' discussions! The construction is a Semitic idiom for an impersonal subject (MHT, 2:447-448). A third person plural subject was used with an active voice as a substitute for an impersonal passive in the Hebrew style of writing, so the identity of the subject is simply impersonal.

I think these three verbs all refer to what God does with fruitless Christians at the Judgment Seat of Christ. 1) Fruitless Christians are gathered together at the judgment of Christians. 2) Fruitless Christians are tested by fire. The fire is a figure of speech for God's holy evaluation of our lives. The fire reveals the worthlessness of our fruitlessness (1 Cor. 3:13). 3) Fruitless Christians are left with nothing because they did not abide in Him and through that abiding produce fruit that possessed eternal value. The sum total of their lives is burned up (καίεται). This is precisely the imagery for the judgment of Christians that Paul uses (1 Cor. 3:13-15). The fruitless Christian suffers loss, but he is saved *"as through fire"* (1 Cor. 3:15).

O Lord, keep me walking and talking with you so that I do not become fruitless in my life!

GLORIFYING THE GARDENER

Jesus tells us, *"By this, my Father is glorified"* (John 15:8). The words "by this" (ἐν τούτῳ) are in the emphatic position at the start of the verse. Jesus is referring forward not backward to the upcoming purpose clause. We glorify God in two ways: 1) by producing much (πολὺν) fruit and 2) by being (or becoming) his disciples. Abiding in Christ is the means of producing fruit and being his disciple bringing glory to the gardener.

The second half of the verse is problematic. Jesus is clearly speaking to those already his disciples so how could they glorify the gardener by becoming his disciples? Several translations supply the word "so" which is not in the text thereby turning the second clause into a result of the first clause. Bearing much fruit proves (or shows) that they are true disciples of Jesus is a common way to interpret the verse.

There is also a textual problem with the verb. Is the verb "become" a subjunctive (γένησθε) mood or a future (γενήσεσθε) tense? The manuscript evidence is evenly divided, but it is probably better to take the verb as a future because of the grammatical structure of the passage. Often a purpose clause introduced by "that" (ἵνα) would take the subjunctive. However, this construction has two verbs connected by "and" (καὶ). As such, it is a special case where the first verb is in the subjunctive mood and the second is a future tense. The future tense indicates a further consequence or future result that stands independently of the first one (BD, p.186). Therefore, being a disciple is not a result of bearing fruit but rather a second way to glorify God. We glorify God by bearing much fruit and by being Jesus' disciples. Both are necessary to glorify God.

What does it mean to be/become a disciple? The verb (γίνομαι) is a fairly loose term with multiple meanings. It can mean to come about or take place - to become. It can also mean to "be" as a substitute for the verb "is" (εἰμι). I suggest that the verb used in this context simply acts as the equivalent of "is" or "are" (BAGD, p. 160). We can translate the verse this way. *"By this, My Father is glorified that you bear much fruit and you will continue to be My disciples."*

What is a disciple? Disciples (μαθηταί) are learners or pupils - students and followers of a teacher (BAGD, p. 485). Learners are always learning and never learned. Disciples are continuously in process. Discipleship is a developmental process - a growing way of life - just as fruit growing on a branch is a process. Jesus is not talking about the point of origin but a continuing process. We have been pupils in the past. We are pupils now, and we will be pupils in the future. To return to the analogy of the vine and the branches, discipleship culminates at the end of life when the fruit of our lives is full and luscious thereby glorifying God, the master gardener.

John 15:9-11

Just as the Father loved me,
9 Καθὼς ἠγάπησέν με ὁ πατήρ,
    And I loved you
    κἀγὼ ὑμᾶς ἠγάπησα·
        remain in my love.
        μείνατε ἐν τῇ ἀγάπῃ τῇ ἐμῇ.

If you obey my orders,
10 ἐὰν τὰς ἐντολάς μου τηρήσητε,
    You will remain in my love,
    μενεῖτε ἐν τῇ ἀγάπῃ μου,
        just as I, myself, have obeyed the orders of my Father
        καθὼς ἐγὼ τὰς ἐντολὰς τοῦ πατρός μου τετήρηκα
            and remain in His love.
            καὶ μένω αὐτοῦ ἐν τῇ ἀγάπῃ.

These things I have spoken to you
11 Ταῦτα λελάληκα ὑμῖν
    In order that my joy might be in you
    ἵνα ἡ χαρὰ ἡ ἐμὴ ἐν ὑμῖν ᾖ
    and your joy might be made full.
    καὶ ἡ χαρὰ ὑμῶν πληρωθῇ.

PREACHING POINTS

The passage breaks down neatly into three preaching points. The first is a command to remain in His love. The second tells us how to remain in his love. The third gives us the result of remaining in His love. The central idea summarizes these points.

Central Idea:

1. (v.9)

2. (v.10)

3. (v.11)

Briefly, identify two contemporary life parallels to these verses.

CLP #1

CLP #2

LIVING IN LOVE WITH JESUS

We live in love with Jesus in the same way that Jesus lives in love with the Father. The comparison (καθὼς) is between living "in My love" (ἐν τῇ ἀγάπῃ μου) and living "in His love" (αὐτοῦ ἐν τῇ ἀγάπῃ). The parallels extend to "My orders" (τὰς ἐντολάς μου) and "My Father's orders" (τὰς ἐντολὰς τοῦ πατρός μου); "you keep" (τηρήσητε) and "I have kept" (τετήρηκα); and "you will remain" (μενεῖτε) and "I remain" (μένω).

We live in love with Jesus by keeping His orders. The conditional sentence (ἐάν + a subjunctive) indicates a level of uncertainty with a sense of probability (DM, p.290). The verb translated "keep" (τηρέω) means to hold or follow, so obey the precepts of Jesus as the condition for loving Jesus in an ongoing, personal relationship (NIDNTT, 2:133).

The Aorist tense (τηρήσητε) indicates our keeping of His precepts is a state of being or a series of actions viewed as a single fact (BUR, p.20). The noun translated "commandments" (ἐντολάς) means precepts or orders (BAGD, p.37). Jesus lives in the Father's love because He "has kept" (τετήρηκα) His Father's orders. The perfect tense indicates past action with an ongoing result in present time (BUR, p.37). Jesus has kept and continues to keep His Father's orders giving us an example to keep His orders.

We will abide in Jesus as we hold to His orders. The verb translated "abide" (μενεῖτε) means to remain and carries an indwelling force. The verb (μένω) expresses intimacy, perhaps the closest personal relationship possible (NIDNTT, 3:225-226). We abide in Jesus as He abides in the Father (Jn. 15:10). The Father who abides (μένων) in Jesus does His works (Jn. 14:10). We who are doing (ποιῶν) the will of God live/remain forever (1 Jn. 2:17; μένει εἰς τον αἰῶνα). Life with Jesus is both now and forever which is why, if we claim to abide in Jesus, we must walk as He walked (1 Jn. 2:6).

Abiding equals living. To remain is to live. To live is to love. Jesus invites us to have the same love relationship with Him that He has with His Father.

INEXHAUSTIBLE JOY

Jesus intended us to experience a life of inexhaustible joy. The noun translated "joy" (χαρά) was used 7 times in the upper room that night before the cross (Jn. 15:11 (2x), 16:20,21,22,24, 17:13) but had been used only once in John's gospel prior to that night (cf. Jn. 3:29, MOR, p. 674). Jesus intends His teaching to produce joy in our hearts. The byproduct of abiding in Jesus is an inexhaustible joy.

"These things I have spoken to you so that My joy may be in you, and that your joy may be made full" (Jn. 15:11). *"These things"* (Ταῦτα) looks back to the previous instruction about abiding in Jesus' love by obeying His commands (Jn. 15:10). Jesus emphasizes an inseparable connection between love and obedience throughout His teaching in the upper room. There is a double purpose for abiding in Jesus: 1) that My joy may be in you, and that 2) your joy may be made full.

"My joy" (ἡ χαρὰ ἡ ἐμὴ) is Jesus' own joy, not the joy produced by Jesus (MEY, p. 434). The Son and the Father experienced an inexhaustible joy in their love for one another from eternity past. God was not a lonely God before creation. He was complete in His own happiness. Jesus' joy stood on the twin pillars of eternally abiding in the Father's love and always obeying the Father's commands (Jn. 15:10). The obedience of a slave produces duty, but the obedience of love produces joy, so Jesus' joy is the product of His loving obedience. The happiness Jesus enjoyed with the Father is the happiness He wants us to enjoy with Him. We will experience the same joy He experiences with the Father by abiding in His love through obedience to His commands.

Our joy is filled up to its fullest extent when we commune with God in prayer (Jn. 16:24). The word translated "made full" (πληρωθῇ) means to be filled up or to be completed (BAGD, p. 671). Jesus asks His Father *"that they (us) may have My joy made full in themselves"* (Jn. 17:13). The pronoun is plural and reciprocal (ἐν ἑαυτοῖς). Joy is relational, communal and reciprocal. Joy is not found in isolation. Our joy is filled up as we experience our love with Jesus and with each other.

The tri-unity of God is a community of infinite love and inexhaustible joy. Our friendship with each other is grounded in our friendship with God - Father, Son, and Spirit. Our joy is made complete as we experience the dual community of God and church (1 Jn. 1:3-4). We will not find true happiness in isolation. Our greatest happiness is relational happiness because we were made to enjoy God as we enjoy the people of God united as one in Jesus.

O, Lord, my lack of inexhaustible joy stems directly from my lack of love for you and your people. Open my heart to your joy by opening my heart to your love.

John 15:12-15

This is my command,
12 Αὕτη ἐστὶν ἡ ἐντολὴ ἡ ἐμή,
    That you love one another
    ἵνα ἀγαπᾶτε ἀλλήλους
        just as I have loved you.
        καθὼς ἠγάπησα ὑμᾶς.
Greater love than this no one has,
13 μείζονα ταύτης ἀγάπην οὐδεὶς ἔχει,
    That someone might die willingly
    ἵνα τις τὴν ψυχὴν αὐτοῦ θῇ
        on behalf of his friends.
        ὑπὲρ τῶν φίλων αὐτοῦ.

You, yourselves, are my friends
14 ὑμεῖς φίλοι μού ἐστε
    If you do what I, myself, order you.
    ἐὰν ποιῆτε ἃ ἐγὼ ἐντέλλομαι ὑμῖν.
    I name you no longer slaves,
15 οὐκέτι λέγω ὑμᾶς δούλους,
        Because the slave knows not what his master is doing,
        ὅτι ὁ δοῦλος οὐκ οἶδεν τί ποιεῖ αὐτοῦ ὁ κύριος·
but you I have named friends,
ὑμᾶς δὲ εἴρηκα φίλους,
    because all things
    ὅτι πάντα
        which I heard from my Father
        ἃ ἤκουσα παρὰ τοῦ πατρός μου
    I have made known to you.
    ἐγνώρισα ὑμῖν.

PREACHING POINTS

There are two main preaching points in the text. The first explains the command to love one another. The second preaching point explains what it means to be a friend of Jesus. The central idea of the passage would summarize those two ideas into one principle.

Central Idea:

1. (vs.12-13)

2. (vs.14-15)

Briefly, identify two contemporary life parallels to these verses.

CLP #1

CLP #2

GREATER LOVE

Sacrifice measures the depths of greater love (μείζονα ταύτης ἀγάπην) which is an expression thrown forward in the sentence for emphasis (v.13). Sacrifice is the standard for the love of friends (φίλων), and Christ is the model. Jesus is speaking here of the love among friends, not the broader scope of love that God displays in the sacrifice of Christ for those who are enemies (Rom. 5:7-8). There is no greater love among friends than the love that risks all – even life itself – for another.

The connective translated "that" (ἵνα) takes the place of an epexegetical infinitive (BD, p.202) to explain the demonstrative "this" (ταύτης). Nobody possesses (ἔχει – present tense indicating ongoing love) greater love than the love Jesus describes in the clause that follows. The verb (θῇ) is an aorist subjunctive from τίθημι generally meaning "put, place or lay" something down (BAGD, p.815). What is laid down, in this case, is "his soul or life" (τὴν ψυχὴν αὐτοῦ).

The expression "to lay down his life" is used only by John in the New Testament (Jn. 10:11,15,17,18; 13:37,38; 15:13; 1 Jn. 3:16. There are two possible senses to the expression. The expression meant to risk life rather than sacrifice life in the Greco/Roman world of the first century. However, the Rabbinic Hebrew background, surely familiar to Jesus, used the expression in the sense of actually sacrificing one's life. John uses the Greek expression with a Hebrew meaning which goes all the way back to Isaiah 53:10 (TDNT, 8:155-156). Jesus uses the expression here the same way He uses it in John 10:11 where the "Good Shepherd lays down His life for His sheep." Jesus is not talking about merely risking His life. He is talking about willfully sacrificing His life for His friends (BERN, P.357).

The preposition (ὑπέρ) originally meant "over or above." The imagery was drawn from a person bending over another person to protect him from harm or a shield raised above the head that suffered the blow intended for the person. The preposition used with the genitive can mean either "on behalf of" in the sense of a representative or "in the place of" in the sense of a substitute. The line between representation and substitution often becomes blurred since acting on behalf of a person often includes acting in his/her place. The result is that ὑπέρ often has the sense of ἀντί. Caiaphas uses ὑπέρ in the sense of substitution when he says that one man should die for the whole nation (Jn. 11:50). Clearly, he means a substitutional sacrifice here (NIDNTT, 3:1196-1197). The Good Shepherd sacrificing his life for his sheep is also substitutional. The other gospel writers use ἀντί instead of ὑπέρ in the parallel passages (Mt. 20:28; Mk. 10:45). Jesus is talking about dying in place of the sheep (BERN, p.357). The same is true in the sacrifice of a friend for a friend. To sacrifice life for a friend is not merely to risk life but to willingly die in place of the friend. Here is the greater love of Jesus demonstrated in the lives of His followers.

John will later argue from the greater love to the lesser love in applying this principle to our lives as Christians (1 Jn. 3:16-17). There is a love for brothers in Christ that transcends love for the world. It is the love of friends. We demonstrate this love when we willingly die in place of another Christian. If we would risk our lives for our brothers how can we ignore the material needs of our brothers and call it love? The love of God does not remain in us who follow Christ if we close our hearts to the needs of our friends in Christ!

"Little children, let us not love with word or with tongue, but in deed and truth" (1 Jn. 3:18).

THE OBEDIENCE OF FRIENDS

We don't commonly associate obedience with friendship. We associate affection with friendship and obedience with slavery. A friend is not ordered to obey like a servant. There is no duty among friends, we think. The essence of friendship is voluntary action. Friends can choose how to act while still being accepted as friends. Yet Jesus says, *"You are My friends if you do what I command you"* (John 15:14).

The condition (ἐὰν ποιῆτε) expresses a degree of "reduced probability" (LN, 89.62). It is not certain that we will obey, so it is not certain that we will experience friendship with Jesus. Jesus invites us to be His friends, but the friendship is conditioned on doing what He commands. Doesn't this condition turn us into servants, not friends?

Jesus goes on to explain that He calls us friends and not servants because a servant doesn't know the mind of the Master, but Jesus discloses to us *"all things"* (πάντα) that He has heard from His Father (John 15:15). The obedience of affection rises out of the self-disclosure of friendship. A friend shares the heart behind the command. Our knowledge changes the nature of our obedience. There is an obedience out of love that is an act of voluntary affection. Such obedience is a choice which explains the conditionality of our friendship with Jesus. In His love, He risks making known (ἐγνώρισα) His deepest desires to us, and in our love, we choose to obey His commands. When we choose to obey out of love, we enjoy the affection of friendship that comes from His self-disclosure (CAR2).

Friendship is commonly mutual. Friends usually choose each other but not so with Jesus. Jesus says, *"You did not choose* (ἐξελέξασθε) *Me, but I chose* (ἐξελεξάμην) *you"* (John 15:16). The verbs are both in the middle voice indicating that the choice is a matter of personal interest. We did not choose Him for ourselves, but He chose us for Himself. Jesus chooses us to be His friends. Jesus chooses to disclose Himself to us as His friends. He risks possible rejection to call us His friends. He invites us into His friendship if we choose to obey Him out of love. This is not an election (choosing) to eternal life but an election to friendship. Therefore, a person can be a follower of Christ without being a friend of Jesus thus turning orders into duties and relationship into religion. When we obey out of love, we enjoy the mutual affection of our friendship with Jesus.

How do we know that we love Jesus? We know we love Jesus when we love one another. The teaching on friendship is bracketed by the command to love one another (John 15:12, 17).

If I won't love Jesus' friends, I can't be Jesus' friend!

John 15:16-17

    You did not choose me for yourself,
16 οὐχ ὑμεῖς με ἐξελέξασθε,
But I have chosen you for myself
ἀλλ' ἐγὼ ἐξελεξάμην ὑμᾶς

and I have assigned you
καὶ ἔθηκα ὑμᾶς

> in order that
> ἵνα
>> you, yourselves, would go
>> ὑμεῖς ὑπάγητε
>> and you would produce fruit
>> καὶ καρπὸν φέρητε
>>> and your fruit would remain.
>>> καὶ ὁ καρπὸς ὑμῶν μένῃ,
> in order that
> ἵνα
>> whatever you would ask the Father
>> ὅ τι ἂν αἰτήσητε τὸν πατέρα
>>> in my name
>>> ἐν τῷ ὀνόματί μου
>> he would do for you.
>> δῷ ὑμῖν.

These things I am ordering you for myself
17 ταῦτα ἐντέλλομαι ὑμῖν,
    In order that you love one another.
    ἵνα ἀγαπᾶτε ἀλλήλους.

PREACHING POINTS

I think there are three main preaching points. Jesus chooses. Jesus assigns, and Jesus orders. The central idea should tie these three points together. One of the striking features of the passage is the repetition of ἵνα, introducing two purpose clauses. The expositor must make an interpretive decision about the second ἵνα. Is the second purpose clause subordinate to the fruit bearing or is it parallel to the first purpose clause as I have diagrammed it here. In other words, is the asking dependent on the fruit bearing or the assignment?

Central Idea:

1. (v.16a)

2. (v.16b)

3. (v.17)

Briefly, identify two contemporary life parallels to these verses.

CLP #1

CLP #2

CHOSEN AS FRIENDS

Normally friends choose each other. Mutual choice equals true friendship but not in this case. Jesus is very clear. The "not" (οὐχ) emphatically negates the pronoun "you" (ὑμεῖς) by its position in the sentence. The sense of the verse should be, "it was not you who chose" instead of "you did not choose" (MOR, p.676, fn36). The pronouns are emphatic – "not you chose me, but I, myself chose you" (ὑμεῖς με ἀλλ' ἐγὼ ὑμᾶς). The personal pronouns indicate aggressive love.

The verb "I chose" (ἐξελεξάμην) is the middle voice of the verb ἐκλέγω. The active voice is not used in the New Testament, so the lexical form is ἐκλέγομαι (NIDNTT, 1:536). It is best understood as an indirect middle where the subject acts for himself – out of personal interest or for personal benefit. As such, it is sometimes called an intensive middle (DM, pp.158-159). Jesus says, "I, myself, chose you for myself."

Jesus chose us for Himself. The verb means to pick out from among many options. It implies that the person making a choice – Jesus – is free to choose without coercion (NIDNTT, 1:536). Jesus' choice in this verse is not for eternal life but for personal relationship. He chose us to be His friends. He chose us for Himself.

Our friendship with Jesus began by His initiative, not ours. Our friendship depends not on our choice but His choice. Jesus anchors our relationship with Him in His free choice of us, grounding our friendship in His will not our whims, His faithfulness not our fickleness.

COMMISSIONED

Jesus says, "I appointed you" (ἔθηκα). The verb (τίθημι) is widely used in the New Testament meaning to put or place something, but it can also mean to make, destine or appoint someone (BAGD, pp.815-816). The word is used to describe God establishing the times of history (Acts 1:7); the Holy Spirit making men overseers (Acts 20:28); destining people for salvation (1 Thess. 5:9) and appointing Paul as an apostle (1 Tim. 2:7). The theme running through these examples is God establishing His decisions by His sovereign authority (NIDNTT, 1:477).

There are two purposes for Jesus' appointment indicated by two purpose clauses (ἵνα). First, Jesus appointed us in order that (ἵνα) we would go (ὑπάγητε) and bear fruit (καρπὸν φέρητε). The going stresses mission (GDT, p.860). The fruit bearing stresses conversion of souls for Christ. Why else would we need to go to carry out His purpose in appointing us (MOR, p.676)? The metaphor changes from the vine and the branches (Jn. 15:1-11) to emissaries who go away to produce fruit. The fruit produced is permanent. "Your fruit," Jesus says, "remains" (μένῃ).

Second, Jesus appointed us in order that (ἵνα) we would ask (αἰτήσητε) whatever (ὅ τι ἄν) from the Father in Jesus' name and He would give (δῷ) it to us. The second purpose clause must be coordinate with the first purpose clause not subordinate to it. It is through prayer that God grants the fruit we bear (MEY, p.437). We ask the Father for fruit, and the Father give us what we ask. Prayer is the primary method for bearing fruit.

Going and praying are coordinated for mission!

John 15:18-20

If the world hates you,
18 Εἰ ὁ κόσμος ὑμᾶς μισεῖ,
    You know that it has hated me first over you.
    γινώσκετε ὅτι ἐμὲ πρῶτον ὑμῶν μεμίσηκεν.
        If you were out of the world,
        19 εἰ ἐκ τοῦ κόσμου ἦτε,
            The world would love its own
            ὁ κόσμος ἂν τὸ ἴδιον ἐφίλει·
                but because you are not out of the world
                ὅτι δὲ ἐκ τοῦ κόσμου οὐκ ἐστέ,
                but I, myself, have chosen you for myself out of the world,
                ἀλλ' ἐγὼ ἐξελεξάμην ὑμᾶς ἐκ τοῦ κόσμου,
                    on account of this, the world is hating you.
                    διὰ τοῦτο μισεῖ ὑμᾶς ὁ κόσμος.

Remember the word which I myself spoke to you,
20 μνημονεύετε τοῦ λόγου οὗ ἐγὼ εἶπον ὑμῖν·
    A slave is not greater than his master.
    οὐκ ἔστιν δοῦλος μείζων τοῦ κυρίου αὐτοῦ.
        If they persecuted me,
        εἰ ἐμὲ ἐδίωξαν,
            They will also persecute you
            καὶ ὑμᾶς διώξουσιν·
        If they observed my word,
        εἰ τὸν λόγον μου ἐτήρησαν,
            they will also observe yours.
            καὶ τὸν ὑμέτερον τηρήσουσιν.

JOHN 15

PREACHING POINTS

There are two main preaching points. The first explains the antagonism of the world for those who follow Jesus. The second main point is a command to remember an important spiritual principle of all followers of Jesus. The central idea of the message should summarize these twin ideas into one over arching principle.

Central Idea:

1. (vs.18-19)

2. (v.20)

Briefly, identify two contemporary life parallels to these verses.

CLP #1

CLP #2

A FAULT LINE WITH THE WORLD

The result of abiding in Jesus is that we are not abiding in the world. The contrast is sharply black and white - no gray allowed. The result of not abiding in the world is that the world hates us. Jesus said, *"If the world hates you, you know that it has hated Me before you"* (John 15:18). The word "know" could be a command instead of a statement (BERN, 2:491). Facing the hatred of the world, Jesus commands us to know they hated Him first (πρῶτον), either first in time or first in importance. Our union with Jesus establishes a fault line with the world leading us to expect persecution from the world.

Jesus states two reasons why the world hates us. The first reason is that Jesus chose us for Himself (ἐξελεξάμην - middle voice). *"I chose you out of the world, because of this the world hates you"* (John 15:19). Three times Jesus uses the same prepositional clause "out of the world" (ἐκ τοῦ κόσμου) in this one verse. *"If you were out of the world the world would love its own; but because you are not out of the world, but I chose you out of the world, because of this the world hates you."*

The preposition "out of" (ἐκ) can indicate either origin or separation (BAGD, p. 234). The first clause expresses origin - often used in the sense of family origin. If our birth family is the world, the world would love us. We are part of the world so why would they not love us? However, we are not out of the world in terms of our birth family any longer. We originate from Jesus. We have a new birth family (point of origin) as those who abide in Jesus. Our birth family rests in His choice - electing love. He chose us "out of the world." The final clause indicates separation. The world is the place from which Jesus separates us by His choice to become part of His birth family. The world hates us because Jesus chose us for Himself.

The second reason the world hates us is that they do not know God the Father. *"But all these things they will do to you for My name's sake because they do not know the One who sent Me"* (John 15:21). Ignorance of God the Father leads to persecution of the Son and His followers. Ignorance of the nature of God leads to failure in recognizing Jesus. When people don't know who God is, they cannot know who Jesus is. Jesus has said that to know God the Father you must know Jesus (John 14:6, 9). Now Jesus reverses the truth - to know Jesus you must know God the Father.

Intimacy with Jesus precludes intimacy with the world. If I am intimate with the world, I cannot be intimate with Jesus. If I am intimate with Jesus, I cannot be intimate with the world. The world will notice the difference and hate me for it. The question is: If I am not hated by the world is it because they do not see any difference in me?!

LOYAL LOVE

Loyalty to Christ leads to loyalty to Christians. Jesus places the jewel of loyal love in the setting of persecution. We as His servants are not greater than Him (see John 13:16), so we should expect to receive the treatment He receives. "If they persecuted Me, they will persecute you; if they kept My word, they will keep your word" (John 15:20). Both conditions are assured to be true (DM, p.287). The first condition is a prediction while the second approximates a promise.

About whom is Jesus speaking? The verbs all have third person plural subjects. They persecuted (ἐδίωξαν), and they will persecute (διώξουσιν). They kept (ἐτήρησαν) His word, so they will keep (τηρήσουσιν) the word of His followers. Some think the distinction between the subjects is a distinction between the crowds who persecute and certain individuals who become disciples (GDT, p.862). It seems better to understand these clauses as general statements leading to a general principle (MEY, p.437). We can tell who follows Jesus by how they treat Jesus' followers.

The verb "to keep" (τηρέω) often means to pressure, protect or guard when the object of the verb is a person or the church. However, a common meaning when the object is impersonal is to observe or fulfill. This second usage of the word is very common in John. The verb occurs twenty-seven time in John, 1 John and Revelation to speak of Christian action (TDNT, p.142-144). Jesus has just said that the one who keeps (τηρῶν) His commandments is the one who loves Him (John 14:21). The present tense indicates ongoing observance of Jesus' commandments. Obedience is the language of loyal love.

There is a surprising contrast (BD, p.149) between "My word" (τὸν λόγον μου) and "your word" (τὸν ὑμέτερον). The second λόγον is implied by the article τὸν, so the contrast is between "My" and "your" word – the word of His followers. Our word is different than His word, but if we are following His word, then our word should reflect His word. Therefore, all who observe His word should also observe our word. If we are observing His word, then we will observe the word of others who follow Him. Observing the word of others who follow Jesus is an act of loyal love to them because of Him.

We should expect persecution from all who reject Jesus. We can expect loyal love from all who obey Jesus. We stand together in the cause of Christ.

John 15:21-25

But all these things they will do
21 ἀλλὰ ταῦτα πάντα ποιήσουσιν
    To you
    εἰς ὑμᾶς
    because of my name,
    διὰ τὸ ὄνομά μου,
        because they do not know the one who sent me.
        ὅτι οὐκ οἴδασιν τὸν πέμψαντά με.
    If I had not come and spoken to them,
22 εἰ μὴ ἦλθον καὶ ἐλάλησα αὐτοῖς,
Sin they would not own
ἁμαρτίαν οὐκ εἴχοσαν·
        but now they possess no excuse
        νῦν δὲ πρόφασιν οὐκ ἔχουσιν
            concerning their sin.
            περὶ τῆς ἁμαρτίας αὐτῶν.

The one who detests me also detests my father.
23 ὁ ἐμὲ μισῶν καὶ τὸν πατέρα μου μισεῖ.

    If I did not do the works among them which no other did,
    24 εἰ τὰ ἔργα μὴ ἐποίησα ἐν αὐτοῖς ἃ οὐδεὶς ἄλλος ἐποίησεν,
Sin they would not own
ἁμαρτίαν οὐκ εἴχοσαν·
        but now they have also seen and detested
        νῦν δὲ καὶ ἑωράκασιν καὶ μεμισήκασιν
            both me and my Father.
            καὶ ἐμὲ καὶ τὸν πατέρα μου.
        But in order that the word might be completed
        25 ἀλλ' ἵνα πληρωθῇ ὁ λόγος
            which was written in their law
            ὁ ἐν τῷ νόμῳ αὐτῶν γεγραμμένος
                they detested me for no reason.
                ὅτι ἐμίσησάν με δωρεάν.

JOHN 15

PREACHING POINTS

The central idea of the passage equates hatred of the Son with hatred of the Father. The reasons for the world's hatred are explained in the repeated expression, "sin they would not own." Each time the phrase is the apodosis to a conditional sentence. There are two conditions for owning sin – the words and the works of Jesus. These are the two main preaching points of the passage giving reasons why hatred of Jesus is hatred of the Father.

Central Idea: (v.23)

1. (vs.21-22)

2. (vs.24-25)

Briefly, identify two contemporary life parallels to these verses.

CLP #1

CLP #2

PRESUMPTUOUS SIN

Presumptuous sin is scary! Presumptuous sin incurs a greater guilt - a deeper culpability - than ordinary sin. A person sins presumptuously when he knowingly and constantly rejects truth to confidently and willfully commit sin.

Jesus said, *"If I had not come and spoken to them, they would not have sin, but now they have no excuse for their sin"* (John 15:22). He is not saying that a person would have been sinless if Jesus had not come. All of us are sinners. Jesus is speaking about the specific sin of conscious unbelief. Jesus came. Jesus spoke the truth. People saw Him. People heard the truth, and people rejected Him and His message. Those people "have sin." The verb translated "have" (εἴχοσαν) means to hold it, grip it or own it! It is conscious sin. They own it without excuse.

Jesus goes on to say, *"If I had not done among them the works which no one else did, they would not have sin; but now they have both seen and hated Me and My Father as well"* (John 15:24). People not only willfully rejected Jesus' message, but they confidently rejected Jesus' works. They "have seen" (ἑωράκασιν) and "hated" (μεμισήκασιν). The verbs are perfect tense verbs indicating a "seeing" and "hating" that are ongoing into the present moment. Presumptuous sin not only owns the sin but carries the rejection forward without remorse leading to the judgment of God.

The Old Testament Law distinguished between ordinary sin and defiant sin (Numbers 15:30), defining defiant sin as blasphemy! Presumptuous sin is a special category of sin leading to greater culpability for sin. Jesus told the Pharisees that he came to help those who were blind to see and cause those who see to become blind. The Pharisees claimed they were not blind so Jesus retorted, *"If you were blind you would have no sin (you wouldn't own it); but since you say, 'we see,' your sin remains"* (John 9:41).

When we present the message and the works of Jesus to people, they become culpable for their choice. We become, as Paul says, *"the smell of death"* or *"the smell of life"* to them (2 Cor. 2:16). A person who knows all about Jesus and still rejects Jesus has greater guilt than one who never hears or knows. On a broader scale, when I know the truth and willfully choose to reject the truth, I am guilty of presumptuous sin. The Psalmist David wrote: *"Keep back your servant from presumptuous sins; let them not rule over me; ... Let the word of my mouth and the meditation of my heart be acceptable in your sight, O Lord"* (Psalm 19:13-14).

Beware of presumptuous sin. Lord, keep from it!

THE MOST HEINOUS HATE CRIME

The crucifixion was the most heinous hate crime of all time. The perpetrators not only hated Jesus, but they hated God because of Jesus. Hatred of the infinite can only lead to an infinite judgment. Jesus said, "The one who is hating me also is hating my Father" (John 15:23).

The word for "hate" (μισέω) means to abhor or detest. A permanent, inner hostility turned Jesus into the enemy (NIDNTT, 1:555). The present tense participle (μισῶν) and the present tense indicative (μισεῖ) indicate ongoing hostility. The hostility of the human heart drives us to sin against God. Sin is the expression of a will that detests Christ because He exposes our sin. Yet God loved us as sinners (Rom. 5:8). Christ teaches us to love our enemies as He loved us (Mt. 5:43-44).

God used human hostility toward Christ to carry out His plan to save His enemies (John 15:25). The hatred of humans took place "in order that" (ἵνα) the word might be fulfilled (πληρωθῇ). The connective (ἵνα) becomes imperatival in this context (MOU, p.144-145). The Word of God had to be fulfilled – a divine necessity – because the cross culminated God's plan to save His enemies. However, the imperatival nature of the hatred does not negate human responsibility even as the hatred fulfills God's plan (MEY, p.439, fn3).

The words of David, the songwriter, were in Jesus' mind when He said, "They hated without cause" (Ἐμίσησάν με δωρεάν). David had written about his woes, "Do not let those who are wrongfully my enemies rejoice over me; nor let those who hate me without cause wink maliciously" (Ps. 35:19). Jesus sees these words as messianic, fulfilled in the hatred of the crucifiers.

The word "without cause" (δωρεάν) literally means gift. Jesus says "they hated me as a gift." Their hatred was a present that required no payment in return. The hatred was free – gratis (BAGD, p.210) and so without cause. They did not hate Jesus because of anything He had done but purely as a gift to Him for who He was.

God used the hate of the world to produce the gift of His love. Humanity's enmity spawned heaven's salvation. God wove the abhorrence of sinful humans into His plan to redeem humanity like an artist weaves flawed strands into a glorious masterpiece. The intertwining of man's hate-filled choices with God's sovereign plan produced salvation for us.

John 15:26 – 16:4

 At the time the legal helper comes
26 Ὅταν ἔλθῃ ὁ παράκλητος
  Whom I, myself, will send to you from the Father
 ὃν ἐγὼ πέμψω ὑμῖν παρὰ τοῦ πατρός,
  The Spirit of truth
 τὸ πνεῦμα τῆς ἀληθείας
   who from the Father goes out,
  ὃ παρὰ τοῦ πατρὸς ἐκπορεύεται,
that one will witness concerning me
ἐκεῖνος μαρτυρήσει περὶ ἐμοῦ·
 but you, yourselves, also witness,
27 καὶ ὑμεῖς δὲ μαρτυρεῖτε,
  Because from (the) beginning you are with me.
 ὅτι ἀπ' ἀρχῆς μετ' ἐμοῦ ἐστε.

These things I have spoken to you in order that you might not be scandalized.
1 Ταῦτα λελάληκα ὑμῖν ἵνα μὴ σκανδαλισθῆτε.

 They will cause you to be expelled from the synagogues
2 ἀποσυναγώγους ποιήσουσιν ὑμᾶς·
  But an hour comes
 ἀλλ' ἔρχεται ὥρα
   that anyone who kills you
  ἵνα πᾶς ὁ ἀποκτείνας ὑμᾶς
    will presume he is offering worship to God.
   δόξῃ λατρείαν προσφέρειν τῷ θεῷ.
 And these things they will do
3 καὶ ταῦτα ποιήσουσιν
  Because they have not known the Father nor me.
 ὅτι οὐκ ἔγνωσαν τὸν πατέρα οὐδὲ ἐμέ.

But these things I have spoken to you
4 ἀλλὰ ταῦτα λελάληκα ὑμῖν
 In order that
ἵνα
   at the time their hour might come
  ὅταν ἔλθῃ ἡ ὥρα αὐτῶν
 you may recall them that I, myself, said to you.
 μνημονεύητε αὐτῶν ὅτι ἐγὼ εἶπον ὑμῖν.
   But these things I did not say to you from (the) beginning,
  Ταῦτα δὲ ὑμῖν ἐξ ἀρχῆς οὐκ εἶπον,
    Because I was continuing to be with you.
   ὅτι μεθ' ὑμῶν ἤμην.

JOHN 15

PREACHING POINTS

The expositor must make a choice here. John 15:26-27 may be taught separately or connected to what follows in John 16:1-4. The connection between the two sections is strong enough to tie them together as one. Jesus is summarizing the second half of John 15 with these verses. The central idea focuses around Jesus' intention that we not be scandalized by what happens to us in this world as we witness for Him. The promise of the Spirit, the knowledge of what is coming and the comfort in recalling Jesus' words form the three main preaching points.

Central Idea: (v.1)

1. (vs.26-27)

2. (vs.2-3)

3. (v.4)

Briefly, identify two contemporary life parallels to these verses.

CLP #1

CLP #2

OUR SPECIAL FRIEND

Jesus promised us a special friend who is called alongside us to help in our time of need (John 15:26). The word "paraclete" (παράκλητος) is hard to translate fully but is best understood as a legal friend, not a spiritual comforter (MOR, pp. 662-666). What does Jesus tell us about our special friend?

1. He is our personal friend, not an impersonal force. The word "spirit" (πνεῦμα) is neuter in gender leading some to imply that the Spirit of God is an influence or force. However, the pronoun used (ἐκεῖνος) is masculine, and the closest antecedent is πνεῦμα not παράκλητος. The pronoun indicates personality. Jesus consistently uses a personal masculine personal pronoun when speaking about the Holy Spirit (John 14:26; 16:8,13,14) proving that He is a person not merely a force.

2. Jesus sends Him to us from the Father. Jesus says that the Holy Spirit is the one *"whom I, myself, will send to you from the Father."* The pronoun is emphatic (ἐγὼ πέμψω). Jesus had said earlier that He would ask the Father to give us a special friend (John 14:16). What the Father gives, the Son sends. Our friend is the answer to Jesus' prayers for us; the gift of our heavenly Father; and the commissioned representative of the Son.

3. He is the Spirit who speaks the truth. Jesus calls Him "the Spirit of Truth" (τὸ πνεῦμα τῆς ἀληθείας). The genitive - "of the truth" - is best understood as an objective genitive. He is the Spirit who communicates the truth. We need a legal friend to speak the truth at all times even when the truth might be unpleasant or inconvenient for us.

4. Our friend proceeds from the Father. Twice Jesus uses the prepositional phrase "from the Father" (παρὰ τοῦ πατρὸς) in this verse. The preposition is often used for Jesus coming from God (John 7:29; 16:27), so the Spirit and the Son both come from the Father. The verb translated "proceed" (ἐκπορεύεται) should not be understood in terms of eternal procession in this verse but rather in the sense of proceeding from the Father for a specific work. The use of the preposition παρὰ instead of ἐκ supports this understanding. The Spirit, as our friend, continues the work of Jesus, as our friend, and both come to us from the Father. All three persons of the Trinity are intimately involved with our lives.

5. He points people to Jesus. Jesus says that *"He will testify"* (μαρτυρήσει) *about Me."* The verb means to bear witness to, to speak well of, someone (BAGD, p. 493). The most important role our special friend has in our lives is to point us constantly to Jesus. The Spirit of God is the shy member of the Trinity. He does not call attention to Himself but prefers to work backstage - behind the scenes - to magnify Jesus (John 16:14). Any work on earth that is truly Spirit directed, Spirit-energized and Spirit stimulated will emphasize Jesus Christ over the Holy Spirit.

AVOIDING THE BAIT STICK

Why did Jesus warn us about suffering and persecution in this world? He wanted us to expect hardship so that we might *"be kept from stumbling"* (John 16:1). It is a purpose clause introduced by ἵνα, and the verb is the passive form of a word (σκανδαλισθῆτε) from which we get our English word "scandal." Jesus warns us so that we will not be scandalized by the sufferings we experience in life.

The noun originally referred to a stick of wood that kept open a deadfall trap for small animals (NIDNTT, 2:707). The bait stick held up a rock or a log which would crush the prey when the bait stick was dislodged. The word later came to mean a stone or other obstacle over which a person tripped and fell.

The verb meant "cause to sin" (to fall) and in the passive meant being led into sin through unbelief or apostasy (BAGD, p. 752). The connection to apostasy is important in the passive. The verb meant to fall away from what was once believed or to be misled from the truth (NIDNTT, 2:708). A professing Christian is scandalized when pressure entices him to fall away from the truth he once clung to by faith.

In the parable of the soils, the seed that fell on the rocky soil sprouted quickly (Mt. 13:20-21). The person received the gospel with joy, *"yet he has no root in himself, but is temporary, and, when affliction or persecution arises because of the word, immediately he falls away"* (σκανδαλίζεται). Pressure (θλίψεως) causes the person to strike the bait stick in his agitation and be crushed by the enemy's trap.

Jesus predicted that there will come times of persecution (θλῖψιν) when Christians will be hated. *"At that time, many will fall away (σκανδαλισθήσονται) and will betray one another and hate one another"* (Mt. 24:9-10). The lies that God promises us prosperity and popularity are the bait sticks of Satan leading many to fall away from Christ.

Avoid the bait stick! How? We must remember Jesus' warning that suffering, pressure, and persecution will come to us (John 16:4) so we will be prepared to face the hardships with faith. As the saying goes, "forewarned is forearmed." The best defense against the scandal of suffering is to expect the suffering. If we are not prepared for hardship, we will fall away and cause others to stumble with us.

After Jesus told the disciples that He would suffer and be killed, Peter vehemently objected. Peter told Jesus not to think this way (Mt. 16:21-22). Bad things wouldn't happen to Jesus because God wouldn't let them happen. I recognize my own false trust in this same bait stick many times. Peter was the epitome of positive thinking. Jesus called him, "Satan," and said that Peter was a bait stick in Satan's trap because he was not setting his *"mind on God's interests but on man's"* (Mt. 16:23).

Lord, help me to avoid the bait stick by expecting pressure in this world and by keeping my mind on your interests instead of mine!

JOHN 16

John 16:5-7

But now
5 νῦν δὲ
    I am going away
    ὑπάγω
        To the one who sent me,
        πρὸς τὸν πέμψαντά με,
and not one out of you all asks me
καὶ οὐδεὶς ἐξ ὑμῶν ἐρωτᾷ με·
    where are you going?
    ποῦ ὑπάγεις;

But
6 ἀλλ'
    Because I have spoken these things to you
    ὅτι ταῦτα λελάληκα ὑμῖν
Grief has filled up your heart.
ἡ λύπη πεπλήρωκεν ὑμῶν τὴν καρδίαν.

But
7 ἀλλ'
    I, myself speak the truth to you,
    ἐγὼ τὴν ἀλήθειαν λέγω ὑμῖν,
It is better for you that I, myself, go away.
συμφέρει ὑμῖν ἵνα ἐγὼ ἀπέλθω.
    For if I do not go away,
    ἐὰν γὰρ μὴ ἀπέλθω,
        The legal friend will not come to you,
        ὁ παράκλητος οὐκ ἐλεύσεται πρὸς ὑμᾶς·
    but if I go,
    ἐὰν δὲ πορευθῶ,
        I will send him to you.
        πέμψω αὐτὸν πρὸς ὑμᾶς.

PREACHING POINTS

The adversatives strikingly stand out in this section. An opening statement after each adversative leads into the point Jesus is making. There are three main preaching points. First, Jesus expresses his disappointment that no one asks where He is going. Second, Jesus notes that they are experiencing grief. Third, He promises that it is better for Him to leave. These three preaching points should be developed as spiritual principles. The central idea would summarize the three main preaching points.

Central Idea:

1. (v.5)

2. (v.6)

3. (v.7)

Briefly, identify two contemporary life parallels to these verses.

CLP #1

CLP #2

USING JESUS VERSUS FOLLOWING JESUS

Jesus has more users than followers in the church today. We use Jesus to sanctify our success and stimulate our worship experiences. Blinded by our self-interests, we often seek a Jesus who serves our needs and promises our prosperity. Our hearts grow restless and bored unless the sermon shows us quickly how Jesus can meet our specific needs now - today - at this moment! We care more about our earthly Jesus than our heavenly Lord.

Jesus saw these tendencies in His first disciples as well. He wistfully said, *Now I am going to Him who sent Me; and none of you asks Me, 'Where are you going?'* (John 16:5). Yet Peter had just asked Jesus that very question only a few hours earlier (John 13:36). How do we harmonize the two verses? What is the question Jesus longs to hear from us?

Some have suggested that the answer is in the present tense of the verb "ask" (ἐρωτᾷ) as if Jesus was saying that no one (οὐδεὶς) was asking Him the question at that precise moment. He was not thinking of what Peter said hours earlier that evening. However, such a solution seems a bit disingenuous, as if Jesus cared more about the timing of the question than the heart of the questioner.

Jesus knew Peter had asked the question that Peter cared about instead of asking the question Jesus wanted Peter to care about. The words are the same, but the intent is so very different. Peter didn't care about the destination of Jesus only that he felt abandoned by Jesus, and it led to a false bravado in his infamous pledge. The disciples were devastated that Jesus was leaving them (John 16:6). They were not interested in the plans of Jesus only the loss they feared for themselves. They only cared about the problems for them not the purposes of the Lord (MOR, pp. 695-696).

We, too, seek selfish answers for life on earth not serious inquiries to understand the glories of our Lord in heaven. Like a child whose father is leaving us to go to work, we often ask "Where are you going?" The father will not be present to play with us! Our intent in asking is selfish. How different is the question of a lover who wants to know all the details about where and what, because of love for the one leaving, not merely the loss of personal presence.

Jesus cares more about the heart of the questioner than the form of the question. A follower of Jesus wants to know everything there is to know about Him and His eternal purposes even if the knowledge is not immediately applicable to his earthly situation. A user of Jesus only cares to know what will meet his problems in that specific moment and cares little to know about anything that is not an immediate life app!

What drives our questions shows the shallowness - or depth - of our relationship with Jesus.

ABSENT BUT PRESENT

Jesus raises a perplexing question in the minds of the disciples. Why is it better for Jesus to leave them than to stay with them? Up until now, He has walked and talked with them; taught them and showed them how to live; and encouraged and strengthened them with His presence. How could it possibly be better for their friend and teacher to leave them now? Yet Jesus said it. It must be true.

"I tell you the truth; it is to your advantage that I go away; for if I do not go away, the Helper will not come to you; but if I go, I will send Him to you" (John 16:7). Grammatically, the clause *"that I go away"* (ἵνα ἐγὼ ἀπέλθω) is the subject of the verb *"it is to your advantage"* (συμφέρει). The verb carries commercial overtones of profitability (MM, p. 598). Jesus says it is profitable, or expedient, for them that He go away.

John only uses the term two other times in his gospel (John 11:50; 18:14), and both times it comes from the lips of Caiaphas, the High Priest. The words of Caiaphas give us the first clue to a partial answer. *"It is expedient* (συμφέρει) *for you that one man die for the people"* (John 11:50). It is better - more profitable - that Jesus goes away because He goes away to die so they might live.

The self-absorbed disciples did not grasp the greater purposes behind Jesus' departure. Jesus had come to die. The cross was God's purpose for Him from before time began. He was also leaving them so the Holy Spirit, the Helper, could come. The Spirit's purpose in coming was to glorify Christ, but the Spirit must have a glorified Christ to glorify (John 7:39). The ascension of Jesus following His cross work glorified Him. He left to be glorified, and the Holy Spirit continues to magnify Him as the risen Lord. The glorification of Jesus leads to the empowering of the disciples through the Holy Spirit.

The personal presence of Jesus would eventually hinder the personal growth of the disciples and the expansion of His kingdom on earth. As long as Jesus remained in bodily form, His presence was limited to His physical location on earth. Omnipresent indwelling was only possible if Jesus left them and ascended into heaven as the glorified Christ. It was better for Jesus to depart so that He could always be with them as they scattered around the globe (Mt. 28:20) through the presence of His Helper wherever they might be.

The Holy Spirit does not merely replace the absence of Jesus on earth. He completes His presence in our lives (BERN, 2:504). We can experience the depths of spiritual intimacy with Jesus in our lives because Jesus departed and the Holy Spirit arrived. The Holy Spirit fills our daily lives with the presence of Jesus in ways that would be impossible if Jesus still walked this earth. Thank you, Holy Spirit, for your empowering presence.

John 16:8-11

And when that one comes
8 καὶ ἐλθὼν ἐκεῖνος
He will convict the world
ἐλέγξει τὸν κόσμον
> concerning sin
> περὶ ἁμαρτίας
> and concerning righteousness
> καὶ περὶ δικαιοσύνης
> and concerning judgment;
> καὶ περὶ κρίσεως·

concerning sin on the one hand,
9 περὶ ἁμαρτίας μέν,
> Because they do not believe in me
> ὅτι οὐ πιστεύουσιν εἰς ἐμέ·

concerning righteousness on the other hand,
10 περὶ δικαιοσύνης δέ,
> Because I am going to the Father
> ὅτι πρὸς τὸν πατέρα ὑπάγω
> > and you no longer see me
> > καὶ οὐκέτι θεωρεῖτέ με·

and concerning judgment
11 περὶ δὲ κρίσεως,
> Because the ruler of this world has been condemned.
> ὅτι ὁ ἄρχων τοῦ κόσμου τούτου κέκριται.

JOHN 16

PREACHING POINTS

The passage breaks down neatly around the repeated preposition περὶ. The central idea is stated in the opening sentence. The Holy Spirit convicts the world. Jesus then explains that convicting work of the Holy Spirit in three ways or spheres.

Central Idea: (v.8)

1. (v.9)

2. (v.10)

3. (v.11)

Briefly, identify two contemporary life parallels to these verses.

CLP #1

CLP #2

THE PROSECUTING PARACLETE

Jesus sent the Holy Spirit to *"convict the world concerning sin and righteousness and judgment"* (Jn16:8). The verb translated *"will convict"* (ἐλέγξει) has four possible meanings: 1) to expose; 2) to convict; 3) to reprove; 4) to punish (BAGD, p. 249). The same meaning should be applied to all three targets - sin, righteousness, and judgment - which eliminates #1 and #4. To merely reprove the world seems rather weak so the best understanding is to convict or convince the world.

The Holy Spirit convicts the whole world. He does not convert the whole world. The verb was used in a legal setting meaning "to cross-examine for the purpose of convincing or refuting an opponent" (BERN, 2:506). Jesus says, "I am sending the Paraclete (παράκλητος) to you" (πρὸς ὑμᾶς), in other words to believers, as a legal friend (Jn. 16:7). The Paraclete is our legal friend, but He is also the world's prosecutor.

The prosecutor's role is to prove sin, righteousness, and judgment to the world whether the world changes or not. The prosecutor proves the guilt to the world so the world can see where they stand before God. The guilty verdict has already been pronounced on the world (Jn. 3:18, 36), but the world needs to be convicted of their guilt before they will ever accept a Savior (CAR, p. 139).

The preposition "concerning" (περὶ) which is repeated with all three categories of conviction can simply be understood as an undefined "with regard to" but seems to carry greater weight. It is better translated as "about" indicating that the Spirit convicts the world of the facts about sin, righteousness, and judgment. The conviction does not guarantee the conversion. Conviction is the necessary prerequisite to conversion, but conversion requires regeneration to be complete.

How does the Spirit do His convicting work in the world? He does it, at least partly, through us. Twice in these verses, Jesus uses the second person pronoun, not the third person pronoun showing us that He is addressing the disciples not the world. Jesus sends the Holy Spirit *"to you"* (Jn. 16:7) meaning the disciples. He also addresses the disciples by saying *"and you no longer see Me"* (Jn. 16:10). So Jesus speaks of the work of the Holy Spirit in the world but sends the Holy Spirit to believers transforming believers into the Spirit's conduit to the world (CAR, p. 143).

The Holy Spirit uses us to bring conviction to the world, but He alone accomplishes conviction. This truth simultaneously relieves our pressure and endows us with confidence as we witness. We don't have to convince anyone by ourselves, and yet our words are invested with His convicting power!

GETTING AT THE ROOT OF SIN

The Holy Spirit convicts the world about sin, righteousness, and judgment (John 16:8). The first conviction is manward in emphasis. The second emphasis is Christward, and the third is Satanward. The explanatory clauses point toward the emphasis in each case (John 16:9-11).

First, Jesus says that the Holy Spirit convicts the world *"concerning sin because they do not believe in Me"* (John 16:9). The focus here is manward. The word translated "because" (ὅτι) could be translated "that" indicating the content of the conviction, but it is better understood as the cause or grounds for the sin. Unbelief in Jesus is the grounds for the conviction.

Jesus says "sin" (ἁμαρτίας) not "sins" as the object of the preposition "concerning" (περὶ). The prosecution proves the sin. Sins, plural, are the symptoms, not the disease. Sin, singular, is the disease, and the disease is unbelief in Jesus. The Holy Spirit does not convict people of breaking the "Ten Commandments" except as a means to prove the sin of unbelief. Breaking specific laws are sins but not sin itself. Sin, the heart of the disease, leads to lawlessness, the symptoms of the sickness (1 John 3:4). The Holy Spirit uses the Law to prove sin like a doctor uses an MRI to prove a disease. The disease at the root of all our sins is the sin of unbelief.

The sin of Adam and Eve in eating of the fruit of the forbidden tree (Gen. 3:6) was an act that demonstrated a faithless heart. Unbelief issues in rebellion and leads to lawlessness. Paul wrote, *"Whatever is not from faith is sin"* (Rom. 14:23). Jesus said that people are convicted because they do not believe in Him. The ultimate sin is a sin of omission not commission. The ultimate sin is something we don't do instead of something we do! Not believing in Jesus is the source of all sins.

The Holy Spirit convicts the world individually not collectively. The "world" (κόσμον) is singular. The verb "they do not believe" (πιστεύουσιν) is plural. The Holy Spirit proves sin to the world by proving sin to each individual in the world. The sin of unbelief is individual, not corporate, and the guilt is personal, not collective.

No matter how much good we do in life, the good we do cannot outweigh the one thing we fail to do if we fail to trust Jesus. Sooner or later the unbelief produces sinful actions. Unbelief is the root of sin. Just like a gardener must pull up the weeds by the roots so the Holy Spirit must convict us of our sins at the root. We can do many good works, but, if we do not believe in Jesus, we stand guilty before God's eternal court.

The prosecuting attorney will never rest His case until He proves our guilt leading either to conversion or condemnation.

WHOSE RIGHTEOUSNESS?

The Holy Spirit convicts the world *"concerning sin and righteousness and judgment"* (John 16:8). He clearly convicts the world of the world's sinfulness (John 16:9), but whose righteousness is in view in the second work of the Holy Spirit? He convicts the world *"concerning righteousness because I go to the Father and you no longer see me"* (John 16:10). Is He convicting the world of its own righteousness or Jesus' righteousness?

Some argue that the three convictions must be consistent. The Holy Spirit convicts the world of its own sin, its own righteousness and its own judgment (CAR, p. 141). In order to do this, we must flip the meaning of righteousness to unrighteousness. He convicts the world of its own, sort of, "bad" righteousness. Otherwise, it is argued, we must change the meaning of convict to convince.

There is, however, no great semantic distinction between convict and convince. The verb (ἐλέγξει) has four possible meanings, but convict and convince are considered to be in the same semantic category - "to convict or convince someone of something" (BAGD, p. 249). The work of convicting is the work of convincing.

Each convicting work of the Holy Spirit contains its own explanatory clause. A causal ὅτι is used in each case. The cause for convincing the world about righteousness is the return of Jesus to the Father and the fact that the disciples no longer will see Jesus. So, the explanation for conviction of righteousness is Christological. The risen and ascended Christ is the focus. The Holy Spirit's work is to convince the world of Jesus' righteousness. The resurrection is the proof of His perfection which is why belief in the resurrection is foundational to our salvation.

The world has an inverted view of righteousness. We think we are righteous (Luke 18:9), and Jesus is a sinner (John 9:24). This was how the people in Jesus' world saw it (MOR, p. 698, fn. 20), and it is still the way the world views righteousness today. In one form or another, we consider ourselves good and Jesus not so good - or, at least, measured by our goodness. As Mary Magdalene famously sings in "Jesus Christ Superstar": "He's a man. He's just a man."

We measure Jesus by our goodness instead of measuring ourselves by His goodness. Therein lies a fundamental problem for mankind so the Holy Spirit convinces people that Jesus is "Perfect Righteousness" in human flesh! He is the standard by which we are measured and fall short. Here is the starting point for our salvation. We have no hope of righteousness in ourselves when measured by His perfection, and any attempt to bring Jesus down to our level leaves us hopeless in our unrighteousness. Our only hope for righteousness rests in His perfect righteousness imputed to us by God when we believe (2 Cor. 5:21).

The Holy Spirit convinces us of Jesus' righteousness, so we will not rest our faith in our perfection but His!

A RULER ALREADY CONDEMNED

The Holy Spirit convicts the world concerning judgment, but it is not the judgment of the world that is the focus of the conviction. The Holy Spirit is not bent on convincing the world that they will be judged. He convinces the world that Satan, as the world's ruler, has already been judged. The ruler of this world has been condemned.

Jesus said that the Spirit, when He comes, will convict the world *"concerning judgment, because the ruler of this world has been judged"* (John 16:11). If we are to take the explanatory clause seriously, then the judgment pertains to Satan, not the world. The Holy Spirit convicts the world of its sin, Christ's righteousness and Satan's judgment (John 16:8). Each convicting work has a clause explaining the convicting work.

The verb translated "judged" (κέκριται) is a perfect tense and passive voice verb. The perfect tense is written from the perspective of a future time. Jesus predicts that, by the time the Holy Spirit comes after Jesus' death and resurrection, the ruler of this world "has been judged!" The passive voice tells us that the judgment is done by someone else. On the cross, God judged Satan!

The verb (κρίνω) means to be condemned. It is a legal term indicating a judicial verdict has been reached, usually in an unfavorable sense (BAGD, p. 450). A sentence of condemnation was pronounced on the ruler of the world when Jesus died on the cross. The tables were turned on the malevolent ruler who orchestrated the crucifixion. The one condemned by the world pronounced condemnation on the one condemning Him. The cross was a victory, not a defeat.

The Holy Spirit convinces the world that their ruler has been sentenced by God. Some sinners in this world will respond to the Spirit's message; confess their sin and trust in the righteousness of Christ. Every sinner who is rescued from the clutches of this world's ruler pounds another nail in the coffin of the condemned ruler (GDT, p. 871).

The Spirit convicts people, who consider themselves good, of their badness. The Spirit convicts people, who consider Jesus unrighteous, of Jesus' perfection. The Spirit convicts people, who owe allegiance to the ruler of this world, of his condemnation. Sadly, some will choose to ignore the conviction and to side with the condemned ruler rather than trust the righteous Savior because they cannot accept their own sinfulness. One day, the one condemned by the world will condemn the world, and all will know what the Spirit taught was true. Until then, the Spirit continues to convict the world of sin, righteousness, and judgment.

John 16:12-15

Still many things I have to say to you,
12 Ἔτι πολλὰ ἔχω ὑμῖν λέγειν,
But you are not able to accept at the present moment
ἀλλ' οὐ δύνασθε βαστάζειν ἄρτι·
    But whenever that one comes
    13 ὅταν δὲ ἔλθῃ ἐκεῖνος,
        The Spirit of truth,
        τὸ πνεῦμα τῆς ἀληθείας,
He will lead you
ὁδηγήσει ὑμᾶς
    in the sphere of all truth
    ἐν τῇ ἀληθείᾳ πάσῃ·
        For he will not speak by his own responsibility,
        οὐ γὰρ λαλήσει ἀφ' ἑαυτοῦ,
            but whatever he is hearing he will speak
            ἀλλ' ὅσα ἀκούσει λαλήσει
            and the things that are coming he will report to you.
            καὶ τὰ ἐρχόμενα ἀναγγελεῖ ὑμῖν.

He will glorify me,
14 ἐκεῖνος ἐμὲ δοξάσει,
    Because from me He will receive and report to you.
    ὅτι ἐκ τοῦ ἐμοῦ λήμψεται καὶ ἀναγγελεῖ ὑμῖν.
        All things as much as the Father has is mine
        15 πάντα ὅσα ἔχει ὁ πατὴρ ἐμά ἐστιν·
            For this reason, I said
            διὰ τοῦτο εἶπον
                that from me He receives and reports to you.
                ὅτι ἐκ τοῦ ἐμοῦ λαμβάνει καὶ ἀναγγελεῖ ὑμῖν.

JOHN 16

PREACHING POINTS

Jesus explains two main preaching points about the Spirit of Truth in this section. The Spirit will lead us, and the Spirit will glorify Jesus. The central idea of the message should summarize these two main thoughts. Jesus prefaces His teaching on the Spirit's work by explaining our need to know in the opening clauses. Jesus stresses the Spirit's dependency on the Son and the Son's joint ownership with the Father of all that is communicated by the Spirit.

Central Idea:

1. (v.12-13)

2. (vs.14-15)

Briefly, identify two contemporary life parallels to these verses.

CLP #1

CLP #2

THE BURDEN OF KNOWLEDGE

The more of God we know, the more responsible we are before God for our knowing. The deeper we penetrate into God's truth, the greater is the weight we carry for God's truth. I'm so glad that Jesus understands our limitations and feeds us His truth one bite at a time!

Jesus said, *"I have many more things to say to you, but you cannot bear them now"* (John 16:12). God's revelation is given piecemeal and progressively down through history. Here, Jesus refutes the false notion that only the gospel accounts were inspired. Jesus pre-authenticates the rest of the New Testament Scriptures with these words. More revelation was coming as God progressively revealed Himself in the collection of writings called the New Testament.

Jesus is thinking of more than historical progression with these words. Jesus allows for our spiritual immaturity. He accommodates Himself to our level of spiritual growth. He gives the disciples and, by extension, us the knowledge we can bear at any given time. The verb "to bear" (βαστάζειν) means 1) to carry or 2) to endure (BAGD, p. 137). The word can refer to carrying a literal burden such as a jar of water (Mark 14:13) or the cross (John 19:17). It can also be used figuratively for carrying the cross (Luke 14:27) or the burden of keeping the law (Acts 15:10). We also bear a burden in the sense of enduring the heat of the day ((Matthew 20:12) or enduring the weaknesses of weaker Christians (Romans 15:1).

We, unlike the disciples, have the full canon of Scripture to examine, but we, like the disciples, may not be able to carry the full burden which comes with that knowledge. We may not be able to stand up under the weight of greater knowledge, so Jesus accommodates our weakness as he grows us stronger in the knowledge of His truth. He helps us understand His truth progressively - one bite at a time.

The Spirit of Truth will guide us and teach us (John 16:13) in His truth as we are able to bear the knowledge we need to grow. Jesus doesn't unload His theological dump truck on us all at once. He feeds us daily at His dinner table so we can assimilate His truth into our lives. He illuminates His truth on a "need to know" basis. He teaches us what we need to know when we need to know it and not before we can bear it.

OUR GUIDE ON THE WAY

Jesus said, *"I am the way* (ἡ ὁδὸς) *and the truth* (ἡ ἀλήθεια) *and the life* (ἡ ζωή).*"* Nobody comes to God, the Father, except through Jesus (John 14:6). How can we walk on the way, know the truth and so live eternal life? Jesus promised that the Holy Spirit *"will guide you (us) into all truth"* (John 16:13) so that we can live His life and walk in His way guided by His truth.

The Holy Spirit is responsible to guide (ὁδηγήσει) us (16:13). The verb means to lead or conduct us along the way (BAGD, p. 553). The etymology of the word helps us grasp its significance. It comes from two Greek words - "lead" (ἄγω) and "way" (ὁδός) - and means to "lead on the way" or "to show the way" (TDNT, 5:97). In the Septuagint, the word is used for the *"pillar of fire by night and the cloud by day, to show you the way in which you should go"* (Deut. 1:33). The noun form is used to describe Judas who became an escort (ὁδηγοῦ) for those who arrested Jesus (Acts 1:16).

The Spirit is our guide who escorts us in the way of Jesus by leading us into all truth. There is a textual problem here. He guides us "into" (εἰς) all truth, or He guides us "in" (ἐν) all truth. The translation "into all truth" suggests that He leads us toward the goal of all truth - a goal we will never reach in this life. The translation "in all truth" suggests that the Spirit leads us in the sphere of all truth. The manuscript evidence favors "in (ἐν) all truth" so it is best to understand it this way. The Holy Spirit guides us in the sphere of truth as we walk on the path of Jesus. The way of Jesus is enveloped in truth.

We can make some important applications from this text.

1) The way is a path, not a moment, a life not an event. The leading is gradual as we walk the way.

2) We cooperate with the Spirit as we walk with Him on the way. Our responsiveness to His guiding is faith not works, but it is faith that walks not waits. There are times, of course, when we must wait for the Spirit to show us the way, but, once shown the way, we must walk it.

3) Jesus, and the Spirit walk ahead of us on the way. It is, after all, the way of Jesus. He and His Spirit lead. They guide. They do not push.

4) All truth is God's truth, but we must rely on the Spirit, not our brains, to show us His truth. Reason must always be subject to the Spirit. Experiences must not define truth for us.

5) The Spirit has been guiding God's people into truth for many years now since Jesus returned to His Father. We are the beneficiaries of two thousand years of the Spirit's leading. The Bible is the ultimate repository - the inspired record - of the Spirit's guidance into all truth.

THE SPIRIT – OUR TEACHER

The Holy Spirit performs three functions for the believer (John 16:13-15) parallel to the three functions He performs for the world (16:8-11). With respect to believers, the Holy Spirit will 1) guide (ὁδηγήσει) us (v.13); 2) teach (ἀναγγελεῖ) us (v.13); and 3) glorify (δοξάσει) Jesus to us (v.14).

The clause about the glorifying work of the Holy Spirit is intensive in form (v.14). Literally the text reads, "that one Himself will glorify Me" (ἐκεῖνος ἐμὲ δοξάσει). The glorification test is an important measuring tool for our ministries. Any ministry claiming to be led by the Holy Spirit will not be characterized by an emphasis on the Spirit but by an emphasis on Jesus. The Spirit guides and teaches in a manner that honors Jesus.

The teaching work of the Spirit is mentioned three times (vs.14-15). The verb (ἀναγγελεῖ) also can mean to report, disclose, announce or proclaim (BAGD, p. 51). It is used for Paul's preaching ministry (Acts 20:20,27) in a way synonymous with teaching (διδάξαι). The primary preaching work of the Holy

Spirit is not revelatory, as in disclosing new information, but proclamation, as in announcing truth to us.

Jesus explains the process of proclamation that the Spirit uses. The Spirit receives from Jesus what He teaches to Jesus' followers. The verb is future in verse 14 (λήμψεται) and present in verse 15 (λαμβάνει). It can mean either to take or to receive (BAGD, p. 464). The source of information is Jesus. Twice the phrase "of Mine" - literally "out of Me" (ἐκ τοῦ ἐμοῦ) is used, and, once again, the "Me" (ἐμοῦ) is in its emphatic form showing us that the Spirit's focus is to point us to Jesus.

Jesus explains that He is the source of the Spirit's information because the Father is the source of His information (v.15). Here we see a neuter plural subject, "all things" (πάντα) with a singular verb (ἐστιν) to emphasize that the information being communicated is viewed as a whole mass, not specific individual teachings (DM, p. 165). Jesus is not separate from the Father for they hold all things - all knowledge - in common (John 17:10). The Spirit communicates knowledge in perfect unity with God the Father and God the Son.

The symmetry of the Godhead is perfect. The Spirit communicates what He receives from Jesus who shared in the knowledge of the Father. In this way, the Spirit glorifies the Son who glorifies the Father for they are one (John 17:4-5).

Help me, Lord, always to study your Word on my knees in total dependence on your Holy Spirit to teach me to know you.

John 16:16-22

A little while and you will no longer see me, and again a little while and you will see me.
16 Μικρὸν καὶ οὐκέτι θεωρεῖτέ με, καὶ πάλιν μικρὸν καὶ ὄψεσθέ με.
    So they said, out of his disciples to one another,
17 εἶπαν οὖν ἐκ τῶν μαθητῶν αὐτοῦ πρὸς ἀλλήλους·
        What is this that he says to us
    τί ἐστιν τοῦτο ὃ λέγει ἡμῖν·
            a little while and you no longer see me,
    μικρὸν καὶ οὐ θεωρεῖτέ με,
        and again a little while and you will see me?
    καὶ πάλιν μικρὸν καὶ ὄψεσθέ με;
        And that I am going to the Father?
    καί· ὅτι ὑπάγω πρὸς τὸν πατέρα;
So they continued to say, what is this that he says the little while?
18 ἔλεγον οὖν· τί ἐστιν τοῦτο [ὃ λέγει] τὸ μικρόν;
    We do not know what he says.
    οὐκ οἴδαμεν τί λαλεῖ.

Jesus knew that they were wanting to ask him, and he said to them,
19 Ἔγνω [ὁ] Ἰησοῦς ὅτι ἤθελον αὐτὸν ἐρωτᾶν, καὶ εἶπεν αὐτοῖς·
    Concerning this are you trying to learn with one another that I said,
    περὶ τούτου ζητεῖτε μετ' ἀλλήλων ὅτι εἶπον·
        a little while and you no longer see me,
    μικρὸν καὶ οὐ θεωρεῖτέ με,
        and again a little while and you will see me?
    καὶ πάλιν μικρὸν καὶ ὄψεσθέ με;
Truly, truly I say to you
20 ἀμὴν ἀμὴν λέγω ὑμῖν
    That you will wail and you, yourselves will sing a dirge,
    ὅτι κλαύσετε καὶ θρηνήσετε ὑμεῖς,
        but the world will rejoice
    ὁ δὲ κόσμος χαρήσεται·
    You yourselves will be grieved,
    ὑμεῖς λυπηθήσεσθε,
but your grief will come to be for joy.
    ἀλλ' ἡ λύπη ὑμῶν εἰς χαρὰν γενήσεται.

    Whenever a woman may be giving birth, she has pain,
21 ἡ γυνὴ ὅταν τίκτῃ λύπην ἔχει,
    Because her hour has come
    ὅτι ἦλθεν ἡ ὥρα αὐτῆς·
    but whenever she gives birth to the child,
    ὅταν δὲ γεννήσῃ τὸ παιδίον,
        she no longer remembers the suffering
    οὐκέτι μνημονεύει τῆς θλίψεως

>>>> on account of the joy
>>>> διὰ τὴν χαρὰν
>>>>> that a person has been born into the world.
>>>>> ὅτι ἐγεννήθη ἄνθρωπος εἰς τὸν κόσμον.

> So also you, yourselves, now, on the one hand, have pain
22 καὶ ὑμεῖς οὖν νῦν μὲν λύπην ἔχετε·
But on the other hand, I will see you again, and your heart will be happy
πάλιν δὲ ὄψομαι ὑμᾶς, καὶ χαρήσεται ὑμῶν ἡ καρδία,
>> and your joy no one takes away from you.
>> καὶ τὴν χαρὰν ὑμῶν οὐδεὶς αἴρει ἀφ' ὑμῶν.

PREACHING POINTS

This unit of thought is a bit more complex. The editors of the Nestle/Aland Greek New Testament divide the section into two paragraphs between verse 18 and verse 19. I think it best to take verses 16-22 as a unit of thought for expositional purposes. The theme (of not seeing Jesus but then seeing Jesus again) pervades the entire section. The theme is stressed again in verse 19. Jesus climaxes the unit of thought by stressing they will see him again in verse 22.

I see three main preaching points: 1) verses 16-18. 2) verses 19-20, and 3) verses 21-22. The first preaching point focuses on the confusion we face in grasping the not seeing but seeing principle. The second preaching point stresses that our pain will become joy. The third preaching point looks ahead to the culmination of our happiness in seeing Jesus again. The childbirth illustration leads into the third preaching point. The second and third preaching points are seen in the contrast (the "but") with the sorrow we face today, so I have visually emphasized those statements in the diagram. The central idea would encompass all three preaching points.

Central Idea:

1. (vs.16-18)

2. (vs.19-20)

3. (vs.21-22)

Briefly, identify two contemporary life parallels to these verses.

CLP #1

CLP #2

SEEING JESUS

Seeing Jesus involves more than merely seeing Jesus! Seeing Jesus through the eyes of faith involves spiritual insight, that is to say, insight produced by the Spirit of God. Jesus taught this truth when He said, *"A little while, and you will no longer see Me; and again a little while, and you will see Me"* (John 16:16).

Two different verbs are connected to two time sequences ("a little while"). The first "little while" (μικρὸν) is the interval of time until His death on the cross. After the cross *"you no longer see Me."* The verb (θεωρεῖτε) is in the present, not future, tense which is significant - you see Me no longer. "No longer" (οὐκέτι) does not mean "never again." The action simply stops (BERN, p.513). The seeing, in this case, is sensual in nature. It means to "be a spectator, look at or observe (BAGD, p.360). After the cross, the disciples ceased to see Jesus with their physical eyes for a little while.

The second "little while" is the interval of time between the cross and the resurrection. The adverb "again" (πάλιν) ties the two intervals together negating any identification of this "seeing" with the return of Christ. The two "seeings" are connected closely in time by the adverb. The resurrection appearances are in view here.

A different verb (ὄψεσθέ) is used for resurrection sight, and it is a future tense. This verb replaces the former verb because it is always used in John to emphasize spiritual perception (BERN, p.513). Jesus combines Easter with Pentecost. The resurrection appearances certainly involved physical sight, but, when the Holy Spirit arrived on Pentecost, the understanding was transformed into spiritual insight. The second "seeing" carries this double sense. The Holy Spirit turns physical sight into spiritual insight (TDNT, 5:360).

However, we must be careful not to over spiritualize this spiritual insight as if it is only a spiritual vision without any reference to actual physical sight as some do (MEY, p.451). The post-resurrection appearances of Jesus were bodily appearances verifiable by physical eyes not mere visionary spiritual experiences.

One clue that the physical sight and the spiritual insight are both true is found in the parallel expression where Jesus says, *"After a little while the world will no longer see* (θεωρεῖ) *Me, but you will see* (θεωρεῖτε) *Me"* (John 14:19). The same verb is used in both sightings - the pre-death and the post-resurrection sightings (MOR, p.703) - making a distinction between sight and insight irrelevant in this statement.

Seeing Jesus involves more than merely seeing Jesus but not less than seeing Jesus. The post-resurrection sightings of Jesus were actual physical sightings not merely visionary experiences of faith. The bodily sightings of Jesus were understood by the spiritual insight of the Holy Spirit even as He was actually visible to those who saw Him. Seeing by the eyes of the body and seeing by the eyes of faith converge to form a single sighting protecting our faith from both mysticism and rationalism.

THE BIRTH PANGS OF JOY

Three words for weeping are used in John 16:20. Jesus said, *"Truly, truly, I say to you, that you will weep and lament, but the world will rejoice; you will grieve, but your grief will be turned into joy."* All three words were used for mourning the dead.

The first word for weeping is κλαύσετε. The word was used for expressing the intense emotion of deep sorrow at the death of a loved one. In the Old Testament, it generally indicated the act of wailing as a form of dependence on God instead of an expression of total despair. The second word for weeping is θρηνήσετε. This word was used for a funeral dirge. The bewailing of death was often characterized in public by striking the chest and singing dirges in a loud voice. (NIDNTT, 2:416-420).

The first two words refer to outward expressions of grief, but the third word speaks of inner suffering (BERN, 2:515). *"You will be grieved,"* Jesus said. The word is λυπηθήσεσθε. It is future passive meaning that something outside the person causes the inner grief. The only other time the word is used in John described Peter's feelings when Jesus asked him after the resurrection if he loved Jesus. Peter was grieved (John 21:17).

There is a sharp contrast in the verse which an English translation cannot bring out effectively. The "you" (ὑμεῖς) is emphatically placed at the end of the clause immediately adjacent to "but the world" (ὁ δὲ κόσμος) beginning the next clause. The contrast between you who grieve and the world that rejoices intentionally intensifies the pain of grief for the believer. The joy of the world makes their tears more painful, but, of course, the story does not end with their tears and the world's joy.

Their tears will not merely be replaced with joy. The verb is γενήσεται which means "to be or become." The very event - the cross - that causes their tears will become the event that brings them joy (MOR, p. 705). So today, the symbol of the cross - the source of sorrow - has become the symbol of faith - the source of hope.

The very same event can change pain to joy. Jesus uses the example of childbirth to illustrate the point (v. 21). Birth pangs had long been associated with the coming of the messianic figure in the Old Testament (Isaiah 26:17-18; 66:7-8; Hosea 13:13). Jesus is predicting the birth pangs of the Messianic Age.

Pain is often the precursor to joy in our lives. Suffering on earth leads to the joy of heaven. Our tears at death are the birth pangs of our joy in life with Jesus forever.

John 16:23-24

And in that day
23 Καὶ ἐν ἐκείνῃ τῇ ἡμέρᾳ
    Me you will not question about anything.
    ἐμὲ οὐκ ἐρωτήσετε οὐδέν.

Truly, truly I say to you,
ἀμὴν ἀμὴν λέγω ὑμῖν,
        whatever you request from the Father
        ἄν τι αἰτήσητε τὸν πατέρα
            in my name
            ἐν τῷ ὀνόματί μου
        he will give to you.
        δώσει ὑμῖν.

Until now you have not requested anything
24 ἕως ἄρτι οὐκ ᾐτήσατε οὐδὲν
        In my name
        ἐν τῷ ὀνόματί μου·
request and you will receive,
αἰτεῖτε καὶ λήμψεσθε,
        in order that your joy might be made full.
        ἵνα ἡ χαρὰ ὑμῶν ᾖ πεπληρωμένη.

PREACHING POINTS

The Nestle/Aland Greek New Testament treats these two verses as a stand alone paragraph in the larger section. There are three preaching points in these two verses revolving around questions and requests. The first deals with a coming change in their relationship with Jesus and how it affects their conversation with Him. The second promises a new prayer relationship with the Father. The third explains the purpose for prayer requests that we make to the Father. The central idea should tie these three components together into a single thought.

Central Idea:

1. (v.23a)

2. (v.23b)

3. (v.24)

Briefly, identify two contemporary life parallels to these verses.

CLP #1

CLP #2

TWO KINDS OF ASKING

There are two kinds of asking in our relationship with God. We can ask a question, or we can ask for a favor. We can seek information from God, or we can make a request for God to do something for us. Both kinds of asking are seen in John 16:23. *"In that day you will not question Me about anything. Truly, truly, I say to you, if you ask the Father for anything in My name, He will give it to you."*

The first asking means to ask a question. The verb is ἐρωτήσετε. The word was used to describe conversation, and it generally meant to ask a question of someone in a dialogue between two people in close relationship with each other (NIDNTT, 2:856-857). The implication of the word was to seek information.

Jesus is not referring to prayer in this clause. He refers to John 16:19 where the disciples were asking questions about His teaching. The "Me" (ἐμὲ) is emphatic in form and position as is the double negative (οὐκ - οὐδέν). The disciples would soon experience a change in their relationship with Jesus. He would no longer be present for them to ask questions.

The second asking means to make a request. This is the language of prayer. It is the new medium of communication for the disciples. The clause is introduced by "truly, truly" (ἀμὴν ἀμὴν) which generally starts a new thought. The verb is αἰτήσητε which means to ask for or even demand something from someone (BAGD, p. 25). Whenever the disciples make requests to God, the verb αἰτέω is commonly used. Whenever Jesus asks God anything, the verb ἐρωτάω is used. The verb αἰτέω refers to a suppliant making a request of a superior while ἐρωτάω refers to a person in a relationship of general equality (NIDNTT, 2:857). Prayer, of course, is the language of a suppliant.

A textual problem occurs with placing the phrase "in my name" (ἐν τῷ ὀνόματί μου) in the sentence. Does it modify the asking or the giving? Do we ask in Jesus' name or does the Father give in Jesus' name? Some manuscripts place it after the giving, so there are those who argue that God's answers to our prayers are in Jesus' name making them more certain (MOR, p. 708).

The stronger manuscript evidence is for the asking to be in Jesus' name. The evidence is more diversified across the geographical spectrum for this reading (METZ, p. 248) making it the stronger reading. This reading also fits better in context because the next verse (16:24) clearly associates "in My name" with asking. We are to direct our requests to the Father in the name of Jesus. This is the normal order of prayer for us.

We have a new relationship with God on the basis of the cross. We now have direct access to the Father. The Old Testament believer did not have this experience. It is new because of the mediatorial work of Jesus. The veil between God and us has been torn down. Even for the disciples before the death of Christ, prayer to the Father had been hindered by the presence of the Son. Now they went directly to the Father because the Son's mission was to connect them (and us) with the Father.

Jesus has been accepted so we are accepted in Him. The intimacy of prayer characterizes our relationship with the Father through Jesus.

John 16:25-28

These things I have spoken to you in dark sayings
25 Ταῦτα ἐν παροιμίαις λελάληκα ὑμῖν·
    An hour comes when I will no longer speak to you in dark sayings,
    ἔρχεται ὥρα ὅτε οὐκέτι ἐν παροιμίαις λαλήσω ὑμῖν,
    but I will announce to you with frankness about the Father.
    ἀλλὰ παρρησίᾳ περὶ τοῦ πατρὸς ἀπαγγελῶ ὑμῖν.

In that day you will request for yourself in my name,
26 ἐν ἐκείνῃ τῇ ἡμέρᾳ ἐν τῷ ὀνόματί μου αἰτήσεσθε,
    And I do not say to you
    καὶ οὐ λέγω ὑμῖν
        that I myself will ask the Father on behalf of you
        ὅτι ἐγὼ ἐρωτήσω τὸν πατέρα περὶ ὑμῶν·
            For the Father Himself loves you,
            27 αὐτὸς γὰρ ὁ πατὴρ φιλεῖ ὑμᾶς,
                Because you yourselves have loved me
                ὅτι ὑμεῖς ἐμὲ πεφιλήκατε
                and have believed
                καὶ πεπιστεύκατε
                    that I myself came from the side of the Father.
                    ὅτι ἐγὼ παρὰ [τοῦ] θεοῦ ἐξῆλθον.

I came out from the Father
28 ἐξῆλθον παρὰ τοῦ πατρὸς
    And I have come into the world
    καὶ ἐλήλυθα εἰς τὸν κόσμον·
        Again I am leaving the world
        πάλιν ἀφίημι τὸν κόσμον
            and I am going to the Father
            καὶ πορεύομαι πρὸς τὸν πατέρα.

JOHN 16

PREACHING POINTS

The text breaks into three main preaching points so the central idea should summarize all three. The first preaching point focuses on the confusion we face as we seek to understand Jesus' teachings. The second preaching point emphasizes the reasons we can go directly to the Father in prayer. The statement that the Father loves us is a subordinate clause, yet sometimes, as here, subordinate clauses carry greater preaching weight than normal. The third preaching point explains the incarnation and the ascension.

Central Idea:

1. (v.25)

2. (vs.26-27)

3. (v.28)

Briefly, identify two contemporary life parallels to these verses.

CLP #1

CLP #2

DARK SAYINGS

Jesus returns to His familiar refrain in the upper room discourse - *"these things I have spoken to you."* The repeated phrase (Ταῦτα λελάληκα ὑμῖν) marks out the sections of His teachings (14:25; 15:11; 16:1,4,6,25,33), and John does not use the phrase elsewhere in his gospel (Morris, John, p. 656). Jesus is looking back in this section specifically to His instructions about His departure to the Father (16:16) which had confused the disciples (16:17) leading Jesus to talk about a woman experiencing childbirth (16:21) as an example of grief turned to joy.

Jesus says that He has been speaking in "figurative language" (παροιμίαις) and promises to speak later in plain language (παρρησίᾳ). John uses the word for figurative language (παροιμίαις) to mean "dark sayings" where "lofty ideas are concealed" (BAGD, p. 629). The word is sometimes synonymous with a proverb or even a parable. The LXX uses παροιμία for the title of the Book of Proverbs (Prov. 1:1). It comes from two words παρα and οιμος meaning "beside the path" to indicate a wise saying alongside a truth (NIDNTT 2:756-757).

John, however, uses παροιμία more in the sense of a dark saying or riddle (John 10:6, 16:25,33) in a similar manner to the word "mystery" (μυστήριον) in the other gospel writers. The contrast with speaking plainly (παρρησίᾳ) leads to this conclusion since proverbs were normally quite clear in meaning, unlike riddles or dark sayings. Jesus has been talking about leaving them; His coming sacrifice for them; the hatred of the world, and His going to the Father. He has talked about suffering grief and loss. Surely these are dark sayings for the disciples to hear!

In what sense are these dark sayings? They are dark sayings not because Jesus was intentionally concealing information from them or because they were intellectually incomprehensible words. They were dark sayings because the teachings were emotionally unacceptable. The disciples were not ready to embrace His teachings. The darkness was in them not in Jesus (NIDNTT 2:758).

When will they understand? Jesus predicts that He will speak plainly in the future. The disciples think they understand and tell Him so (16:29), but they do not yet grasp His dark sayings. Jesus speaks plainly in His post-resurrection appearances, but it is not until after Pentecost and the coming of the Holy Spirit that the disciples truly grasp the dark sayings of Jesus (BERN, 2:519). Jesus said as much when He taught that the Holy Spirit would take His words from the Father and "disclose" them to the disciples (16:13-15).

We, too, experience the dark sayings of Jesus when we struggle emotionally to understand and accept our loss, our grief, and our suffering in this life. The deep waters threaten to overwhelm us even though we have the rest of Scripture to bolster our faith. We still need the Holy Spirit as our "Special Friend" to disclose Jesus' dark sayings to us because of the darkness that sometimes shrouds our minds.

Thank you, Holy Spirit, for being our teacher during the dark times of our lives

MY FATHER LOVES ME THIS I KNOW

My Father loves me. He is happy to hear me when I pray. Jesus said, *"In that day you will ask in My name, and I do not say to you that I will request of the Father on your behalf; for the Father Himself loves you, because you have loved Me and have believed that I came forth from the Father"* (John 16:26-27).

The pronoun "himself" (αὐτὸς) is emphatic both by usage (MOU, p. 121) and in position as the first word of the phrase preceding "for" (γὰρ). The verb "loves" (φιλεῖ) indicates ongoing affection in the present tense. It is the only place where John uses φιλέω as opposed to ἀγαπάω in order to communicate God's love for us (BERN, 2:520). While an absolute distinction cannot be maintained between these two verbs, it is generally true that φιλέω implies the idea of human affection more than the higher form of willful love (ἀγαπάω) normally used for God by John.

Jesus says that He does not need to persuade the Father to listen to us because the Father Himself has great affection for us. Jesus does not mean He will never intercede for us or be our advocate with the Father. He means that we do not need Him to be our "go-between" in prayer because we can go directly to the Father. He, Himself, loves us. He, Himself, hears us!

Jesus gives us two reasons for the Father's love. The ὅτι is causal and introduces two perfect tense verbs indicating two reasons the Father loves us. First, He loves us because *"Me, you, yourselves, have loved."* The "me" (ἐμὲ) and the "you" (ὑμεῖς) are both emphatic. The perfect tense tells us that the choice to love (πεφιλήκατε) was a past event (for the disciples) with ongoing results in present time.

The Father loves us because we love His son. This love is different than His love for the world (John 3:16). The affection He feels for those who love His son is an affection He does not feel for those who do not love His son. He loves us in a different way than He loves the world. Like the father who loves a young man because the young man loves his daughter, our heavenly Father loves us because we love Jesus. Our love for Jesus "seals the deal" on His love for us.

The second reason for the Father's love is because we have believed (πεπιστεύκατε) is another perfect tense indicating a past choice with continuing results in the present. This is not a nebulous faith. The content of the faith is defined by "that" (ὅτι) - a content not a causal usage as earlier. We believe that Jesus *"came forth from (παρα) the Father."* the preposition (παρὰ) means "from the side of" (ATR, pp. 579,614). It is not enough to believe that Jesus was born into this world. We must believe that Jesus was sent from the side of the Father. Faith in the pre-existence of Jesus is essential to enjoy the personal love of the Father.

My Father loves me.
This I know.
For my Savior
Tells me so!

John 16:29-33

His disciples said,
29 Λέγουσιν οἱ μαθηταὶ αὐτοῦ·
See, now you are speaking with frankness
ἴδε νῦν ἐν παρρησίᾳ λαλεῖς
and you no longer are speaking in veiled language.
καὶ παροιμίαν οὐδεμίαν λέγεις.
    Now we know
30 νῦν οἴδαμεν
        That you know all things
ὅτι οἶδας πάντα
            and you have no need
καὶ οὐ χρείαν ἔχεις
                that anyone should ask you a question
ἵνα τίς σε ἐρωτᾷ·
        by this, we believe
ἐν τούτῳ πιστεύομεν
            that you came out from God
ὅτι ἀπὸ θεοῦ ἐξῆλθες.
Jesus answered them
31 ἀπεκρίθη αὐτοῖς Ἰησοῦς·
Now you are trusting?
ἄρτι πιστεύετε;
        Look an hour is coming even has come
32 ἰδοὺ ἔρχεται ὥρα καὶ ἐλήλυθεν
            That may be dispersed
ἵνα σκορπισθῆτε
                each one into his own
ἕκαστος εἰς τὰ ἴδια
                and me alone you may leave
κἀμὲ μόνον ἀφῆτε·
                    and I am not alone
καὶ οὐκ εἰμὶ μόνος,
                      because the Father is with me.
ὅτι ὁ πατὴρ μετ' ἐμοῦ ἐστιν.
These things I have spoken to you
33 ταῦτα λελάληκα ὑμῖν
        That in me you might have peace.
ἵνα ἐν ἐμοὶ εἰρήνην ἔχητε.
            In the world you continually have trouble
ἐν τῷ κόσμῳ θλῖψιν ἔχετε·
            but be confidant,
ἀλλὰ θαρσεῖτε,
                I, myself, have conquered the world.
ἐγὼ νενίκηκα τὸν κόσμον.

JOHN 16

PREACHING POINTS

There are three main preaching points. First, the disciples express confidence that they understand and trust Jesus. Second, Jesus corrects their false confidence with the truth about how they will abandon Him. Third, Jesus reassures them with His promise of peace. The "big idea" should summarize these three preaching points to meet a contemporary need.

Central Idea:

1. (vs.29-30)

2. (vs.31-32)

3. (v.33)

Briefly, identify two contemporary life parallels to these verses.

CLP #1

CLP #2

SATAN'S WORK BUT GOD'S PURPOSE

"An hour is coming (ἔρχεται) even has come (ἐλήλυθεν)," but this hour is not merely any hour (John 16:32). This hour is "the" hour! Jesus prayed, *"Father, the hour has come"* (ἐλήλυθεν) for the glorification of the Son (John 17:1, cf. John 2:4; 7:6). The time has arrived for the greatest event in human history to take place. The enmity between the seed of Satan and the seed of the woman (Gen. 3:15) will come to its decisive hour.

Jesus must face this battle alone. The hour has come for the disciples to leave Him alone as they are scattered (John 16:32) each to his own (ἕκαστος εἰς τὰ ἴδια). When we are scattered from the Lord and each other, we individually (each one - ἕκαστος) enter into (εἰς) our own things (τὰ ἴδια). The expression is used for John taking Jesus' mother into his own household (John 19:27). It could be translated "each for himself." The adjective is neuter plural referring to our possessions and our relationships. Our human nature drives us to seek our own personal goals - the matters we control - whenever we abandon the Lord.

The scattering (σκορπισθῆτε) and subsequent abandonment (ἀφῆτε) are introduced by an important conjunction (ἵνα). The conjunction can be translated simply "that" indicating the content of the hour coming upon them, or it could be translated "when you are scattered" (DM, pp. 248-249). However, the original, and most common, use of ἵνα was to introduce a purpose clause. In fact, ἵνα plus a subjunctive verb became "almost the exclusive means of expressing purpose" (A. T. Robertson, Grammar, p. 982). The scattering (σκορπισθῆτε) and the abandoning (ἀφῆτε) are both subjunctive verbs, so this is best understood as a purpose behind the coming hour.

Jesus used the scattering (σκορπίζει) of the sheep as a description of Satan's work (John 10:12) when the hireling shepherd abandons his sheep. Jesus didn't abandon His sheep, but Satan did scatter the sheep in this hour. Satan's scattering work must be seen as within the scope of God's overall purpose. In the garden at His betrayal, Jesus said, *"All this has taken place to fulfill the Scriptures of the prophets. Then all the disciples left him and fled"* (Mt. 26:56). Zechariah had predicted the scattering when he wrote, *"Strike the Shepherd that the sheep may be scattered'* (Zech. 12:7). God intended to scatter the sheep leaving Jesus alone to battle Satan on the cross. The apparent victory of Satan was part of God's sovereign plan for the disciples.

Satan's work accomplishes God's purpose. We cannot understand, sometimes, why Satan seems to win in this world. We scatter, like the disciples, to pursue our own things in life feeling like Satan has won; forgetting, in our despair, that God has a purpose even in the victories of Satan!

PEACE UNDER PRESSURE

Jesus draws three contrasts between our two spheres of life followed by one command built on one reality that clarifies our perspective. He concludes his instruction in the upper room with the familiar refrain, *"These things I have spoken to you"* (John 16:33; cf. 14:25; 15:11; 16:1,4,6,25,33). This expression (ταῦτα λελάληκα ὑμῖν) is not used elsewhere in John (MOR, p. 656).

"These things I have spoken to you, so that in Me you may have peace. In the world you have tribulation, but take courage; I have overcome the world" (John 16:33).

There are three contrasts in this verse.

In Me vs. In the world
Peace vs. Pressure
Might have vs. Have

We simultaneously experience two spheres of life. The "in Me" (ἐν ἐμοὶ) sphere of life should be the dominant reality. The expression is emphatic both in position and form. The "in the world" (ἐν τῷ κόσμῳ) sphere of life, while seemingly the dominant reality, should be secondary, not primary.

The two spheres of life are characterized by two contrasting experiences. In Christ, we have peace (εἰρήνην) while in the world we have pressure (θλῖψιν). We can experience peace and pressure at the same time because we live in both spheres simultaneously. Peace and pressure co-exist in the life of every Christian. Peace is not the absence of pressure. We can have peace in the middle of our troubles.

Pressure in the world is a given while peace is a possibility. Jesus says, *"you have"* (ἔχετε) pressure in this world. The present tense indicative verb implies an ongoing reality. Jesus says, *"you might have"* (ἔχητε) peace in Him. The present tense verb is subjunctive in mood which is the mood of probability or possibility. Peace is not guaranteed unless the following command is obeyed.

The command is to *"take courage"* (θαρσεῖτε) which follows a strong adversative *"but"* (ἀλλὰ). Peace under pressure comes from courage under fire. We can have courage because Jesus has established a new reality for us. *"I have overcome the world."* The "I" (ἐγὼ) is not only emphatic but contrastive as well. "I" contrasts strongly with "you" (ATR, p. 677). We might have expected Jesus to say, "Take courage. You have overcome the world." He doesn't say that, of course, because the victory is not in us but in Him.

John 16:33 is the only time John uses the verb νικάω in the Gospel, but he uses it six times in 1 John (cf. 1 John 5:4) and 17 times in Revelation (MOR, p. 714, fn 82). Here in John 16:33 the verb is a perfect active indicative form (νενίκηκα) indicating that Jesus has already won the the victory with ongoing results for us. He states this before the cross so certain is He of the results of the looming battle. Jesus faced the cross with the assurance of total victory. He goes to the cross with confidence that He will conquer the enemy despite the horror He faces in battle.

We must take courage in His victory. We have victory because He has victory. We are conquerors because He is conqueror (Romans 8:37). We can have peace under pressure because we take courage that He is the conqueror.

JOHN 17

John 17:1-5

    These things Jesus said
    Ταῦτα ἐλάλησεν Ἰησοῦς
        And after raising his eyes to look into the heaven, he said,
        καὶ ἐπάρας τοὺς ὀφθαλμοὺς αὐτοῦ εἰς τὸν οὐρανὸν εἶπεν·

Father, the hour has arrived, make your son gloriously great,
πάτερ, ἐλήλυθεν ἡ ὥρα· δόξασόν σου τὸν υἱόν,

    in order that the son might make you gloriously great,
    ἵνα ὁ υἱὸς δοξάσῃ σέ,
        just as you gave Him authority over all flesh
        2 καθὼς ἔδωκας αὐτῷ ἐξουσίαν πάσης σαρκός,
            In order that all whom you have given to him
            ἵνα πᾶν ὃ δέδωκας αὐτῷ
                He might give to them eternal life.
                δώσῃ αὐτοῖς ζωὴν αἰώνιον.

And this is eternal life
3 αὕτη δέ ἐστιν ἡ αἰώνιος ζωὴ
    That they might know
    ἵνα γινώσκωσιν
        you, the only true God
        σὲ τὸν μόνον ἀληθινὸν θεὸν
        and Jesus Christ whom you have sent.
        καὶ ὃν ἀπέστειλας Ἰησοῦν Χριστόν.

I myself have made you gloriously great
4 ἐγώ σε ἐδόξασα
    Upon the earth
    ἐπὶ τῆς γῆς
        after having finished the work
        τὸ ἔργον τελειώσας
            which you gave to me that I should carry out
            ὃ δέδωκάς μοι ἵνα ποιήσω·

Even now, you, Father, make me gloriously great,
5 καὶ νῦν δόξασόν με σύ, πάτερ,

    Alongside yourself
    παρὰ σεαυτῷ
        with the glory
        τῇ δόξῃ
            which I possessed
            ᾗ εἶχον
                before the world was
                πρὸ τοῦ τὸν κόσμον εἶναι
            with you.
            παρὰ σοί.

JOHN 17

PREACHING POINTS

The repeated expression, "Father, make me (your Son) gloriously great" in verses 1 and 5 are bookends for this opening segment of Jesus' prayer. These bookends should form the basis of the central idea of the message. There are four main preaching points that support Jesus' request for glory. Three preaching points are in between the two requests for glory and one follows the second request for glory.

Central Idea:

1. (v.1b-2)

2. (v.3)

3. (v.4)

4. (v.5)

Briefly, identify two contemporary life parallels to these verses.

CLP #1

CLP #2

THREE GIFTS AND THREE GROUPS

Jesus uses the verb "to give" (δίδωμι) 3 times with respect to 3 distinct groups of people in the opening words of His great prayer (John 17:2). The order of the groups is significant despite the fact that some English translations reverse the order of the final two groups. Each group is a subset of the previous group in the sequence (BD, p. 77).

Father, the hour has come; glorify your Son, that the Son may glorify you, since you gave to Him authority over all flesh, in order that the ones you have given to Him, He may give to them eternal life.

The first group is "all flesh" (πάσης σαρκός). The Father gave (ἔδωκας) to Jesus authority over all flesh. The genitive is best understood as an objective genitive so "all flesh" is the object of authority (ATR, p. 500). The noun "flesh" (σαρκός) is used to stress the weakness of humanity. All (πάσης) humans in fleshly weakness are given to the Son to be under His authority.

The second group of people is the Father's gift to the Son. This group is a subset of all flesh. "You have given" (δέδωκας) them to Me, Jesus prays. The verb is from the same root (δίδωμι), but it is a perfect active indicative. The Father gave these people to the Son in the past with ongoing results. The disciples were already given to the Son by the Father. The group is identified by the neuter, singular construction "the ones whom" (πᾶν ὅ). The neuter singular construction is used for a group of people characterized by some defining quality (MHT, 3:21). The quality that defines this group is that they are a gift from the Father to the Son.

The same construction is used by Jesus in John 6:37 where He says: *All that (πᾶν ὅ) the Father gives (δίδωσίν) Me will come to Me, and the one who comes to Me I will certainly not cast out.* Everyone given by the Father will come to the Son. It is sufficient for anyone coming to Christ that they are given by the Father.

The Son gives (δώσῃ) eternal life to the ones (αὐτοῖς) who have been given to Him by the Father. The pronoun (αὐτοῖς) views the collective group (πᾶν ὅ) individually. Jesus gives eternal life individually to each one who has been given to Him as part of the collective group. Eternal life is our personal gift from Jesus.

Jesus' words are, perhaps, the strongest statement about sovereign election in Scripture. There is no way to escape the grammatical argument of the passage. All who have been given at some time in the past to the Son receive the gift of eternal life from the Son.

Thank you, Jesus, that I am doubly gifted! I am the Father's gift to you, as incomprehensible as that may be, and I receive your gift of eternal life with joy. Secure forever as the Father's gift to you, I appreciate with joy your gift to me.

DEFINING ETERNAL LIFE

Eternal life is not merely endless existence. Eternal life is knowing God. Jesus said *This is eternal life, that they may know You, the only true God, and Jesus Christ whom You have sent* (John 17:3). To know God is the essence of eternal life. Here is the simplest definition of life forever.

The ἵνα introduces a clause in apposition to eternal life (ATR, p. 1078). Eternal life is explained by what follows ἵνα in the verse. It is not that the knowledge of God gives life or is the way to have eternal life. When I know God my life is transformed into eternal life for life is found in God and death, by definition, is separation from God (MOR, p. 720).

Knowing God is a present tense verb (γινώσκωσιν) indicating that our knowledge starts now. We have eternal life right now as we live on earth because we know God now. We are not merely awaiting eternal life in the age to come. We enjoy it now. The aspect of the present tense indicates a continuous, ongoing knowledge, even increasing knowledge. Certainly, our knowledge of God is growing until it culminates in perfect knowledge in the age to come, but we are still living eternally right now because we know God right now.

The contents of our knowledge are laid out in almost a confessional form (MEY, p. 461). The substance of our knowledge is the knowledge of two persons - God and (καὶ) Jesus Christ. One must know both to live eternally. To know a person, we must know certain propositions about that person before we can know the person relationally.

God is the only (μόνον) God. He is solitary, unique. There are no other gods to know if you want eternal life. God is the true (ἀληθινὸν) God (1 John 5:20). He is trustworthy, genuine, authentic and real. He is not spurious or fake like the gods (idols) of this world. To know those gods is not to enjoy eternal life for those gods do not live forever.

John 17:3 is the only place where Jesus calls Himself by His compound name - Jesus Christ. Some suggest that the verse is an editorial comment by John rather than part of Jesus' prayer. However, the second person verb "whom you sent" (ἀπέστειλας) and the personal pronoun "you" (σὲ) both prove that Jesus is praying these words. He is Jesus (God saves) and Christ (The Anointed One) who was sent by God so we could know God.

Eternal life is knowing God now and forever!

MY GLORY

Glory, His and His Father's, dominated the mind of the Savior on His last night on earth. Twice Jesus requests the Father to glorify Him as He faces death on the cross (John 17:1, 5). The verb translated "glorify" (δόξασόν) is the imperative of request (BUR, p. 80) stressing the seriousness, even demand, of His petition to the Father. Prayer can be demand when Father and Son are one!

The second request (17:5) is different than the first in two ways. Jesus said, "glorify me" (v.5) rather than "glorify the Son" (v.1) stressing the personal relationship rather than His role as Savior. Jesus focused on His past glory (v.5) versus His future purpose to glorify the Father (v.1).

And you, Father, glorify me now, alongside yourself, with the glory which I used to have alongside you before the world was.

"I want back what I gave up," Jesus cries out. He wants to be glorified "with the glory" (τῇ δόξῃ), an instrumental use of the dative case (MOU, p. 44). The glory is the instrument for glorification. "Glory" means magnificence, radiance or splendor (BAGD p. 204). He is asking to be honored with the magnificence or splendor He once had with the Father.

"I want back what I had with you," Jesus pleads. "The splendor I had alongside yourself" (παρὰ σεαυτῷ) is the glory Jesus seeks. The preposition (παρὰ) with the dative (σεαυτῷ) means "by the side of, beside or near" (BAGD, p. 610). This is the glory Jesus experienced alongside the Father on the throne of Heaven in eternity past.

"I want back what I used to have," Jesus demands. The verb (εἶχον) is in the imperfect tense. It is best understood as a customary imperfect indicating repeated, ongoing action in the past (BUR, p. 12). Jesus possessed the majestic radiance of Almighty God in His pre-incarnate life. Now He looks forward to a return to that state of splendor He once enjoyed.

"I want back what I once enjoyed before creation," Jesus requests. The present articular infinitive (τοῦ ... εἶναι) is a temporal use indicating the time of the glory that He seeks again (ATR, p. 978). The prepositional phrase "before the world" (πρὸ ... τὸν κόσμον) further defines the time. The preposition (πρὸ) combined with the articular infinitive (τοῦ ... εἶναι) often substitutes for another preposition (πριν) meaning "before" (ATR, p. 1074). He wants His glory from before the cosmos existed when the angels worshiped Him in all His splendor.

Jesus gave it all up to save us, but He got it all back when His cross work was completed. Paul gives us a divine commentary on the prayer of Jesus in Philippians 2:5-11 which was likely an early confessional hymn. Jesus laid aside His glory and humbled Himself to die on the cross. God, then, exalted Jesus giving Him a name above all names so that at the name of Jesus every knee will one day bow, and every tongue will one day confess Jesus Christ is Lord, to the glory of God the Father. The circle of John 17:1 and 17:5 is complete on that glorious day.

Lord, be glorified in me today!

John 17:6-8

I have disclosed your name to the human beings
6 Ἐφανέρωσά σου τὸ ὄνομα τοῖς ἀνθρώποις
    Whom you gave to me out of the world.
    οὕς ἔδωκάς μοι ἐκ τοῦ κόσμου.

    They were yours
    σοὶ ἦσαν
        and to me you gave them
        κἀμοὶ αὐτοὺς ἔδωκας
            and your word they have obeyed.
            καὶ τὸν λόγον σου τετήρηκαν.

Now they have come to understand
7 νῦν ἔγνωκαν
    That all things
    ὅτι πάντα
        which you have given to me
        ὅσα δέδωκάς μοι
            are from you.
            παρὰ σοῦ εἰσιν·
                because the words
                8 ὅτι τὰ ῥήματα
                    Which you have given to me
                    ἃ ἔδωκάς μοι
                        I have given to them
                        δέδωκα αὐτοῖς,

    and they accepted
    καὶ αὐτοὶ ἔλαβον
        and they really understood
        καὶ ἔγνωσαν ἀληθῶς
            that I came out from you,
            ὅτι παρὰ σοῦ ἐξῆλθον,
            and they believed
            καὶ ἐπίστευσαν
                that you, yourself, sent me.
                ὅτι σύ με ἀπέστειλας.

JOHN 17

PREACHING POINTS

The editors of the Nestle/Aland Greek New Testament treat these verses as a separate paragraph – a unit of thought. The central idea should express that Jesus revealed God to those God gave to Him, namely believers. There are three main preaching points which follow this big idea. All three preaching points express some aspect of our response to the disclosure of God by Jesus.

Central Idea:

1. (v.6b)

2. (v.7-8a)

3. (v.8b)

Briefly, identify two contemporary life parallels to these verses.

CLP #1

CLP #2

GIVEN FOR KEEPS

We are the Father's love gift to His Son. Jesus says of the disciples - we are included by extension - that the Father gave (ἔδωκάς) them to Jesus out of (ἐκ) the world (John 17:6). The disciples were separated out of the unbelieving world to be the Father's love gift to Jesus (MEY, p. 463).

Jesus goes on to say, "*they were yours*" (σοὶ ἦσαν) and "*to me*" (κἀμοὶ) "*them*" (αὐτοὺς) "*you gave*" (ἔδωκάς). The disciples were the Father's possession first. They had belonged to the Father before they belonged to the Son. The word translated "yours" (σοὶ) is a possessive use of the dative case (MOU, p. 120).

Jesus had said earlier that those who do not hear God's words are not from God (John 8:47). God separated the disciples from those who do not hear His words so that they become God's possession. The Father chooses us for Himself and gives us to His Son, so we are secure in His love! We are His before we even come to Christ.

"*They have kept your word*," Jesus says. The "word" is singular (λόγον) because Jesus is not talking about specific words but His essential message as a whole. The disciples have failed to keep His words at times, just as we do, but they have kept His Word, His essential message, and not left the faith. Jesus had said earlier, "*If anyone loves Me, he will keep my word* (singular, λόγον); *and my Father will love him, and we will come to him and make our abode with him* (John 14:23). We fail in specific areas, but we are secure in His sovereign love, so we keep His essential message.

The disciples have kept (τετήρηκαν) His word. The verb is in the perfect tense. Robertson calls it a "durative - punctiliar" act (ATR, p. 895) in that a process preceded a complete state. The disciples have lived through a process of keeping that has led to a culmination of that process in their current state. The verb "to keep" (τηρέω) means to hold or preserve. It can also mean to observe or obey (BAGD, pp. 814-815).

Spiritual testing leads the disciples to hold on to His word. Jesus makes this affirmation in advance of their abandonment at the cross the next day. Jesus is absolutely certain that the consummation of their testing will be the keeping of His word. How can Jesus be so certain about the end result given the obvious fickleness of their faith? Jesus can be certain because they are the Father's possession - a love gift to the Son.

The fickleness of our faith never negates the faithfulness of His love! We are given for keeps!

John 17:9-12

I myself am asking on behalf of them,
9 Ἐγὼ περὶ αὐτῶν ἐρωτῶ,
    Not on behalf of the world am I asking
    οὐ περὶ τοῦ κόσμου ἐρωτῶ
    but on behalf of those whom you have given to me,
    ἀλλὰ περὶ ὧν δέδωκάς μοι,
        because they are yours,
        ὅτι σοί εἰσιν,
            and all mine are yours
            10 καὶ τὰ ἐμὰ πάντα σά ἐστιν
            And yours are mine,
            καὶ τὰ σὰ ἐμά,
            and I have been made gloriously great in them.
            καὶ δεδόξασμαι ἐν αὐτοῖς.

And I am no longer in the world,
11 καὶ οὐκέτι εἰμὶ ἐν τῷ κόσμῳ,
    And they, themselves are in the world,
    καὶ αὐτοὶ ἐν τῷ κόσμῳ εἰσίν,
    and I am coming to you.
    κἀγὼ πρὸς σὲ ἔρχομαι.
    Holy Father, keep watch over them in your name
    πάτερ ἅγιε, τήρησον αὐτοὺς ἐν τῷ ὀνόματί σου
        which you have given to me,
        ᾧ δέδωκάς μοι,
    in order that they might be one just as we (are one).
    ἵνα ὦσιν ἓν καθὼς ἡμεῖς.

As long as I was with them
12 ὅτε ἤμην μετ' αὐτῶν
    I myself kept watch over them
    ἐγὼ ἐτήρουν αὐτοὺς
        In your name
        ἐν τῷ ὀνόματί σου
            which you have given to me,
            ᾧ δέδωκάς μοι,
    and I guarded,
    καὶ ἐφύλαξα,
        and no one out of them has been ruined
        καὶ οὐδεὶς ἐξ αὐτῶν ἀπώλετο
            except the son of ruination
            εἰ μὴ ὁ υἱὸς τῆς ἀπωλείας,
                in order that the Scripture might be satisfied.
                ἵνα ἡ γραφὴ πληρωθῇ.

JOHN 17

PREACHING POINTS

We see three main preaching points in this diagram based upon Jesus' changing presence with respect to His followers. First, Jesus identifies the relational foundation for His prayers on our behalf. Second, Jesus makes His request specific. Third, Jesus expresses His faithfulness in guarding His followers while He was with them. The central idea should encompass all three of these preaching points.

Central Idea:

1. (vs.9-10)

2. (v.11)

3. (v.12).

Briefly, identify two contemporary life parallels to these verses.

CLP #1

CLP #2

SECURED BY HIS PRAYERS

Jesus asks the Father to protect us. Can we be any more secure than that?! Twice Jesus will use the term "keep" (τηρέω) in His prayer for us. He asks the Father to guard us in God's name (John 17:11), and He asks the Father to protect us from the Evil One (John 17:15). Jesus establishes the keeping work of the Father by the intercessory prayer of the Son making us eternally secure in God.

Jesus prays for us, not the world. *I ask on their behalf; I do not ask on behalf of the world, but of those whom You have given Me; for they are Yours* (John 17:9). Jesus certainly loves the whole world. Why does He not pray for the whole world? Because He prays here as our High Priest seeking the protection of those He is leaving in this world. Such a prayer can only be prayed for believers, not the world.

Jesus uses the verb "ask" (ἐρωτῶ) twice in this verse. It is a present tense verb best understood as a progressive present indicating action in progress at the time (BUR, p.7). The verb (ἐρωτῶ) can mean either to ask a question or to make a request on behalf of another (BAGD, pp. 311-312). Here Jesus is requesting the Father's help on our behalf. Jesus uses another verb (αἰτέω) for the prayers of men but always uses ἐρωτάω for His prayers because it implies equality with the Father (MOR, p. 549, fn 48).

The preposition περί with a genitive object usually means "about or concerning" (BAGD, p. 644). However, περί can be used, as it is here, as a substitute for ὑπέρ meaning "on behalf of" (BD, p. 121). The third use of περί connects the relative pronoun "whom" (ὧν) with its antecedent "their" (αὐτῶν) making both prayer requests for the same group - His followers (ATR, p. 721).

The Father has given (δέδωκας) us to Jesus. The perfect tense expresses past action with a current result (BUR, p. 37). Even before the cross, the Father had already given the disciples to the Son. They were His even as they abandoned Him! We too, are His, the love gift of the Father to the Son, even though we don't always live as if we are His.

We had belonged to the Father before the Father gave us (ἔδωκας) to the Son (John 17:6). The gift is not a handoff as we no longer belong to the Father because Jesus says to the Father "they are yours" now (σοί εἰσιν). The verb (εἰσιν) is a present progressive tense. "They continue to be yours, Father, even as they are mine," Jesus asserts (John 17:10).

Our eternal security is secured by the gift of the Father and the prayers of the Son so that we need never worry about our eternal destiny.

ONE IN HIS NAME

Jesus' departure from this world is the grounds for His prayer. He said, *"I am no longer in the world; and yet they themselves are in the world, and I come to you, Holy Father"* (John 17:11). The verbs, "I am" (εἰμί), "they are" (εἰσίν), and "I come" (ἔρχομαι), are all in the present tense. Jesus prays as if His pending departure has already happened. He prays from the vantage point of heaven.

God's holiness in contrast with the world's unholiness is the grounds for guarding us. *"Holy Father, keep them in Your name,"* Jesus prays. The vocative, "Holy Father" (πάτερ ἅγιε) is important. Jesus' prayer request to the Father to guard His followers is in perfect harmony with God's holiness and because of the world's unholiness. We remain in this unholy world, so we need a Holy Father to keep us in His name. We can pray, *"Hallowed be your name"* (Mt. 6:9) only as the Holy Father keeps us in His name (MEY, p. 466).

"Keep" (τήρησον) is an imperative of request. It carries the force of urgency and intensity without carrying the force of command (DM, p. 176). The verb (τηρέω) means "to keep watch over, guard" or even "hold" and "preserve" someone (BAGD, p.814). Jude later addresses his letter to those who are *"beloved in God the Father and have been kept* (perfect tense of τηρέω) *for Jesus Christ"* (Jude 1:1). Here is the answer to Jesus' request in John 17!

Jesus asks the Father to *"keep them in Your name, which You have given Me"* (John 17:11). The textual problem illustrates the dilemma for interpreters. Is Jesus talking about the disciples being given to Him - some manuscripts use the pronoun ους - or is He talking about the name being given to Him - other manuscripts read ᾧ. The disciples are certainly given to Jesus (John 17:9), but the more difficult reading is preferred in this verse. The gift in this verse (and verse 12) is the name. The antecedent of "which" (ᾧ) is "the name" (τῷ ὀνόματι). The Father gives the Son His name thereby indicating that God's essential nature is seen in the Son (BER, 2:559).

The purpose of keeping them in His name is unity - oneness - "that (ἵνα) they may be (ὦσιν) one (ἕν) even as we are." We are one as the Father and Son are one (see John 10:30). Jesus extends His prayer for unity to all His followers including us in verse 21. The verb (ὦσιν) is a present active subjunctive from εἰμί. It is the verb of existence - to be not to become. Jesus does not pray that we become one. He prays that we continue to be one. The number one (ἕν) is neuter in gender suggesting an essential oneness - a unit. We exist as one just as the Father and Son exist as one (MOR, p. 727).

Our oneness is not organizational but organic, not ecumenical but spiritual. We are a unit in the name of Jesus. Jesus speaks of an ontological unity here. We do not create unity. We participate in a unity He created. All who genuinely name His name share His life, so we participate in His oneness no matter what human name we use to describe ourselves. We are kept in His name because we share in His nature. God will never fail to keep us one although we may fail to live as one.

IN HIS CUSTODY

Jesus keeps all He receives. The pattern of protection Jesus demonstrated for His disciples is the pattern we can expect for ourselves. *"While I was with them, I, myself, was keeping them in your name which you have given to me, and I guarded them, and no one out of them was lost except the son of lostness, that the Scripture might be fulfilled"* (John 17:12).

The two verbs for protection used here are probably used synonymously (NIDNTT, 2:135), although there could be slightly different shades of meaning between the two. The first verb (ἐτήρουν) meant to keep watch over or preserve (BAGD, p. 814) while the second verb (ἐφύλαξα) meant to guard or defend (BAGD, p. 868). Both verbs could be used for prisoners under the custody of guards.

The first verb (ἐτήρουν) is an Imperfect tense indicating action in progress or repeated action. Jesus was keeping watch over the disciples until this moment of His prayer for them. The second verb (ἐφύλαξα) is an Aorist tense indicating a summation of His guardianship. They were in His custody, and He lost no one out of the group (οὐδεὶς ἐξ αὐτῶν).

The exception (εἰ μή) was Judas. Jesus describes him as the "son of destruction" (ὁ υἱὸς τῆς ἀπωλείας), an expression drawn from the Hebrew (Semitic) style of writing. The play on words with the previous verb (ἀπώλετο) is hard to bring out in an English translation. Both words come from the same root meaning to ruin or destroy, and Jewish literature associated the word with the destruction of the world at the end of the age (NIDNTT, 1:463). The verb carries a sense of lostness and is used for the lost sheep and the lost coin in Jesus' parables (Luke 15:4, 8). People without God are lost. Lostness is the condition of their souls (NIDNTT, 1:464).

Judas and the "man of lawlessness" (2 Thess. 2:3) are both described as sons of destruction. It is a Semitic idiom like "sons of light" or "sons of darkness." The noun "son" (υἱός) followed by the genitive expresses a quality or characteristic (MHT, 3:207), not a prediction. Jesus stresses that lostness characterizes the condition of Judas more than He stresses lostness as the destiny of Judas (MOR, p. 728). A lost condition will eventually lead to a lost destiny. He is a ruined soul whose end is destruction apart from repentance. Judas is responsible for his choices, but those choices exhibit his characteristic condition as the son of lostness.

Jesus keeps us in His custody. We are "sons of God (υἱοί εἰσιν θεοῦ) being sons of the resurrection" (Luke 20:36). We are not sons of lostness just as the disciples were not! We are children (τέκνα θεοῦ) of God (John 1:12). Jesus holds His children in His custody forever. He will not lose a single one!

John 17:13-16

But now I am coming to you
13 νῦν δὲ πρὸς σὲ ἔρχομαι
    And these things I am speaking in the world
    καὶ ταῦτα λαλῶ ἐν τῷ κόσμῳ
        in order that they might have my gladness
        ἵνα ἔχωσιν τὴν χαρὰν τὴν ἐμὴν
            be made full in themselves.
            πεπληρωμένην ἐν ἑαυτοῖς.

I, myself, have given to them your word
14 ἐγὼ δέδωκα αὐτοῖς τὸν λόγον σου
    And the world detested them
    καὶ ὁ κόσμος ἐμίσησεν αὐτούς,
        because they are not out of the world
        ὅτι οὐκ εἰσὶν ἐκ τοῦ κόσμου
            just as I, myself, am not out of the world.
            καθὼς ἐγὼ οὐκ εἰμὶ ἐκ τοῦ κόσμου.

I am not asking
15 οὐκ ἐρωτῶ
    That you carry them away out of the world,
    ἵνα ἄρῃς αὐτοὺς ἐκ τοῦ κόσμου,
        but that you guard them from the evil one.
        ἀλλ' ἵνα τηρήσῃς αὐτοὺς ἐκ τοῦ πονηροῦ.

They are not out of the world
16 ἐκ τοῦ κόσμου οὐκ εἰσὶν
    Just as I am not out of the world.
    καθὼς ἐγὼ οὐκ εἰμὶ ἐκ τοῦ κόσμου.

JOHN 17

PREACHING POINTS

The central idea is summed up in verse 16. Jesus is focused on our relationship to the world because of our relationship to Him. Three main preaching points develop the theme of the follower of Christ in this world of evil.

Central Idea:

1. (v.13)

2. (v.14)

3. (v. 15)

Briefly, identify two contemporary life parallels to these verses.

CLP #1

CLP #2

PRAYER THAT FILLS US WITH JOY

Jesus prayed to be heard. His prayer in John 17 was not silent but audible. He prayed out loud as the disciples listened. His prayer was for their benefit demonstrating for us that audible prayer leads to joy for those who listen.

How do we know Jesus prayed out loud in John 17? He said, *"These things I am speaking in this world in order that they might possess My joy having been filled up in them"* (John 17:13). The verb translated "I am speaking" (λαλῶ) means to speak in contrast to staying silent. The word referred to the physical act of making sounds in contrast to the inability of a deaf and mute person to make sounds (cf. Mark 7:35; BAGD, p. 463). Jesus prayed out loud not for His benefit or God's, but for the benefit of the disciples who were listening (MEY, 3:467).

"These things" (ταῦτα) that Jesus is saying could refer to the entire discourse (John 13-16), but most likely refer to the prayer itself (John 17). The present tense of speaking (λαλῶ) implies that He is continuing to express "these things" not that He had said "these things" in the past. Jesus was making the following requests to the Father as the disciples listened to Him pray.

- Keep them in your name (v.11)
- That they may be one (v.11, 21)
- Keep them from the Evil One (v.15)
- Sanctify them in truth (v.17)
- That they may be perfected in unity (v.23)
- That they may be with Jesus and see His glory (v.24)

The purpose of Jesus' prayer was that (ἵνα) they, and we by extension (see v.20), might possess (ἔχωσιν) His joy (τὴν χαρὰν τὴν ἐμὴν). What is the joy Jesus wants us to enjoy? It is the joy that Jesus Himself possesses (John 15:11; 16:24). Jesus' joy is the joy of His heart drawn from the obedient communion with the Father. It is the joy of knowing for certain that no matter what happens we are being kept by the Father, protected in His care just as Jesus was kept by the Father (GDT, p. 895). Jesus knew this joy even as He faced the cross. We, too, can experience His joy in the certainty of God's loving care for us.

The joy has filled us and is continuing to fill us up. The verb is a perfect tense (πεπληρωμένην) indicating a past filling with abiding results. The passive participle tells us that God does the filling that we enjoy. We do not fill ourselves with His joy. He makes us full of joy no matter our circumstances in life.

The joy we experience - His joy - is found in ourselves (ἐν ἑαυτοῖς). This joy is a joy we experience in our inner conscious person (BAGD, p. 212). We have an inner joy that comes from hearing Jesus pray for God's loving care sheltering us in this world. Nothing can happen to us outside of God's work of keeping us which produces in us a deep joy in our inner person.

We can follow Jesus' example in prayer for each other. All too often our prayers revolve around our health and wealth. Perhaps if we heard others pray for us as Jesus prayed for us, we would be filled up with Jesus' joy in our inner being! Perhaps if we prayed more for the things Jesus prayed about, we would experience more of the joy Jesus enjoyed!

THE BELIEVER, THE WORLD, AND THE EVIL ONE!

We face a world system (ὁ κόσμος) filled with evil. Often - too often - we wish to escape the evil in this world system, but that is not God's will for us during this age. Jesus intends that we stay in the world so long as the world is not in us. Jesus prays, *"I am not asking that you (Father) remove them from the world but that you might keep them from the evil (one)"* (John 17:15).

Is it evil or the evil one? The articular adjective in the genitive case (τοῦ πονηροῦ) can be taken as either neuter or masculine in gender. Some take it as neuter indicating generic evil that rules this world system (GDT, p.896). The prayer is that we would be kept out of an evil domain. Others understand the adjective as masculine referring to the Evil One - the Devil (MEY, p.467). We are not to be kept out of the evil domain but from the power of the Evil One even as we remain in his domain. This interpretation fits the context better.

We hear an echo from the Lord's Prayer (Mt. 6:13) where Jesus taught us to pray, *"deliver us from the Evil One."* The verb translated "deliver" (ῥῦσαι) is different, and the preposition "from" (ἀπὸ) is different, but the sentiment is parallel. The distinction between prepositions is not significant in this case, and the better contextual interpretation is that Jesus is talking about the Evil One not evil generically in the Lord's Prayer (BER, 2:573).

The preposition "from" (ἐκ) frequently used in John 17 indicates separation from what once had power over us (ATR, p.598). The phrases "from the world" (ἐκ τοῦ κόσμου) and "from the Evil One" (ἐκ τοῦ πονηροῦ) are parallel in John 17:15. Jesus says that we are not removed (ἄρῃς) from the world, but we are separated from the Evil One who controls and dominates the world. John will later write that we have overcome the Evil One (1 John 2:14) who controls the world. *"We know that we are of God and that the whole world lies in (the power of) the Evil One"* (ἐν τῷ πονηρῷ, 1 John 5:19).

Jesus prays that the Father might keep (τηρήσῃς) us from the Evil One. The verb can mean to keep as in "not lose" but is probably better understood as to keep as in "protect" (BAGD, p.815). The expression is only found in one other place in the New Testament - Revelation 3:10 (BER, 2:573). We are kept from *"the hour of testing which is about to come upon the whole world,"* John writes in the Apocalypse. Once again the preposition "from" (ἐκ) is not an expression of motion signifying that we are kept through a period of time. The preposition indicates an absolute keeping - a separation - from the hour of testing coming upon this world. In the same way, we are separated from the power of the Evil One by His protection. The Devil has no power over us!

Jesus asks the Father to protect us from the power of Satan even as He leaves us in the domain of Satan. If Jesus asks the Father for our protection, surely the Father agrees, so we are secure in His keeping that separates us from the power of the Evil One. All who are His are kept by His power!

John 17:17-19

Consecrate them
17 ἁγίασον αὐτοὺς
    In the sphere of truth
    ἐν τῇ ἀληθείᾳ·
        Your word is truth.
        ὁ λόγος ὁ σὸς ἀλήθειά ἐστιν.

        Just as you sent me
18 καθὼς ἐμὲ ἀπέστειλας
        Into the world,
        εἰς τὸν κόσμον,
even so, I have sent them
κἀγὼ ἀπέστειλα αὐτοὺς
    into the world
    εἰς τὸν κόσμον·

    and on behalf of them
19 καὶ ὑπὲρ αὐτῶν
I, myself, consecrate myself,
ἐγὼ ἁγιάζω ἐμαυτόν,
        in order that they, themselves, might be consecrated
        ἵνα ὦσιν καὶ αὐτοὶ ἡγιασμένοι
            in truth.
            ἐν ἀληθείᾳ.

JOHN 17

PREACHING POINTS

Verse 17 expresses the central idea of the section. The focus is on being set apart in the orbit of truth. The two main preaching points in verses 18 and 19 develop what it means to be set apart for God and how Christ sets us apart.

CENTRAL IDEA:

1. (v.18)

2. (v.19)

Briefly, identify two contemporary life parallels to these verses.

CLP #1

CLP #2

SANCTIFIED TO SERVE

Jesus uses the imperative mode to make His request for us to the Father when He says, *"Sanctify (ἁγίασον) them in the truth, your word is truth"* (John 17:17). His request for our sanctification arises out of the reality that we are not part of this world just as He is not part of this world (vs.16). Our otherworldliness leads to hostility from the world system and forms the basis of our sanctification.

Sanctify does not mean to purify which would be the verb καθαρίζω (BAGD, p.387). Sanctify means to set apart for God, to consecrate or dedicate (BAGD, p. 8). The verb was frequently used in the LXX, the Greek translation of the Old Testament, for the sanctifying of priests to serve God and the sanctifying of the sacrifices for the worship of God (NIDNTT, 2:232). The priests and the sacrifices were set apart exclusively for God's use. Purity, of course, is the necessary result of sanctification because that which is sanctified must no longer be profane.

Jesus' sanctification is the basis for our sanctification (vs. 19). Jesus said, *"I sanctify myself (ἐγὼ ἁγιάζω ἐμαυτόν) on behalf of them (ὑπὲρ αὐτῶν) in order that (ἵνα) they, themselves, might be sanctified (ἡγιασμένοι) in truth."* Jesus needs no purification. He sets Himself apart (sanctifies Himself) to carry out the Father's will. He is sanctified to die as our sacrifice for sin - an idea drawn from the Old Testament doctrine of sanctified sacrifices.

The truth found in God's Word is the means of our sanctification. We are sanctified in the sphere of truth (ἐν τῇ ἀληθείᾳ). God sets us apart within the orbit of truth's influence so that truth defines our lives. God's Word is truth. "Your word" has the definite article (ὁ λόγος ὁ σὸς), but "truth" does not have the definite article (ἀλήθεια). The absence of the article is intentional. "Truth" and "Word" are not "convertible" terms (ATR, p. 768). The absence of the article does not make truth indefinite. Truth is qualitative. Truth describes the quality that defines the Word of God. We are sanctified as God's Word permeates our lives with His truth. We become God's as God's Word becomes ours. The more we immerse ourselves in God's Word, the more we set ourselves apart for God's work.

Service is the purpose of sanctification (vs. 18). Just as God sent (ἀπέστειλας) Jesus into this world, so Jesus sent (ἀπέστειλα) us into the world. He was commissioned to die for us, and we are commissioned to live for Him (CAR, p. 193). Jesus' purpose in sanctifying us is to send us out to serve Him in this world.

Jesus prays for our sanctification. He is not praying for our moral purity as much as He is praying for our consecrated service. Moral purity is a corollary to consecration. We are to live holy lives because profane lives render us useless for His service. We are sanctified to serve.

John 17:20-23

But I am not asking concerning them only,
20 Οὐ περὶ τούτων δὲ ἐρωτῶ μόνον,
But also concerning the ones who believe
ἀλλὰ καὶ περὶ τῶν πιστευόντων
    through their word
    διὰ τοῦ λόγου αὐτῶν
  in me,
  εἰς ἐμέ,

in order that they all might be one,
21 ἵνα πάντες ἓν ὦσιν,
    Just as you, Father, (are) in me and I in you,
    καθὼς σύ, πάτερ, ἐν ἐμοὶ κἀγὼ ἐν σοί,
    that they might be in us,
    ἵνα καὶ αὐτοὶ ἐν ἡμῖν ὦσιν,
      in order that the world might believe
      ἵνα ὁ κόσμος πιστεύῃ
      that you, yourself, sent me.
      ὅτι σύ με ἀπέστειλας.

  And the glory
22 κἀγὼ τὴν δόξαν
    Which you have given to me
    ἣν δέδωκάς μοι
    I have given to them,
    δέδωκα αὐτοῖς,
in order that they might be one
ἵνα ὦσιν ἓν
  just as we are one.
  καθὼς ἡμεῖς ἕν·

    I in them and you in me,
  23 ἐγὼ ἐν αὐτοῖς καὶ σὺ ἐν ἐμοί,
In order that they might be completed into one,
ἵνα ὦσιν τετελειωμένοι εἰς ἕν,
  in order that the world might know
  ἵνα γινώσκῃ ὁ κόσμος
    that you sent me
    ὅτι σύ με ἀπέστειλας
    and you loved them
    καὶ ἠγάπησας αὐτοὺς
      just as you loved me.
      καθὼς ἐμὲ ἠγάπησας.

PREACHING POINTS

The striking feature of this section is the repeated use of clauses introduced by ἵνα. Six times ἵνα is repeated in these four verses. The exegetical problem is determining which are major and which are minor clauses as well as which are content and which are purpose clauses. The Central Idea of the passage centers around Jesus prayer for unity. Three times ἵνα is used with the phrase "in order that they might be one." Each time the prayer for unity is repeated, Jesus expands His thought. There are three main preaching points each developing an expanded aspect of the prayer for unity.

Central Idea:

1. (v.21)

2. (v.22)

3. (v.23)

Briefly, identify two contemporary life parallels to these verses.

CLP #1

CLP #2

THE ONE-NESS OF IN-NESS!

Jesus asks the Father that we, as His followers, be one in Him. He asks not only for the disciples but also for those who believe through their message (John 17:20). His heart cry for us is our unity in Him. He prays *"that they all (πάντες) might be one, just as you, Father, (are) in me and I in you, that they, themselves, might also be in us, in order that the world might believe that you, yourself, sent me"* (John 17:21).

There are three clauses introduced by "that" (ἵνα) in this verse. The first two ἵνα clauses express the content of the request while the third ἵνα clause introduces the purpose for the oneness (RIEN, p. 256). It is possible that the second of the two content ἵνα clauses is actually in apposition to the first (DM, p. 249) reinforcing and expanding the content of the request.

Our oneness is God's oneness. We are one as God is one. The expression "just as"(καθὼς) indicates essential oneness, a oneness of nature and purpose. Jesus is not asking for organizational unity, and He is not asking for the uniformity of conformity. The Father and the Son are different yet one. Their oneness controls their differences even as their differences stimulate their love. If God were one but not three, He could not love. If God were three but not one, He could not save. In eternity past, God must be three to have someone to love, and He must be one to be united in the plan of salvation. God's oneness of purpose is grounded in the possession of an inner reality of oneness. It is an ontological unity having to do with the very nature of God's existence. They are different but one, so we, too, are different but one.

The key is the preposition "in" (ἐν). The Father is in the Son, and the Son is in the Father, and we are in both! (plural pronoun -ἡμῖν) Although impossible to fully grasp, our one-ness depends on our in-ness! We cannot be one with someone who is not in Christ. The preposition must not be understood simply as "belongs to" or "with" God. The theological implications are more profound than mere proximity or association (MHT, 3:263). We are only one with each other because we share in the spiritual nature of the triune God. All other unity is not the unity Jesus asks from the Father on our behalf.

The purpose (ἵνα) is to show the world that the Father sent Jesus. The purpose is not exactly, or merely, evangelistic since people can believe that the Father sent the Son without trusting in the Son for personal salvation. However, our unity should be a visible witness to the world. We show the unity of God as we show unity among ourselves. We must not seek merely organizational unity or structural uniformity. The greater witness is spiritual unity of heart despite our differences in form and structure.

Father, help me to live as one with other followers of Jesus even with our differences - especially in our disagreements - to show the world our oneness of heart and purpose in Christ.

LOVED LIKE JESUS

Our unity as Christians demonstrates love, not our love but God's love! Jesus prays in John 17:23 that we might become perfected or completed (ὦσιν τετελειωμένοι) into one (εἰς ἕν). The passive voice tells us God does the perfecting of our unity not us. The preposition "into" (εἰς) as opposed to the more common "in" indicates the purpose or result of a process (BD, p. 111). God's work of uniting believers as one is in a process of completion throughout life.

The purpose of our unity is that (ἵνα) the world might know (γινώσκῃ) true love. The content of the knowledge is introduced by a second "that" (ὅτι). Our unity shows that (ὅτι) God, the Father, sent Jesus (ἀπέστειλας) and loved (ἠγάπησας) the disciples of Jesus. A single "that" (ὅτι) governs both verbs, "sent" and "loved." (MOR, p. 736, fn 69). God's love for us and God's sending of His Son are a unit of thought. The sending of His Son proves the depth of His love for us.

The measure of the Father's love for us is the amount of His love for His Son. The adverb "just as" (καθὼς) compares His love for us to His love for His Son. Jesus says, *"you loved them, just as you loved me."* Both verbs are in the Aorist tense indicating an action that is undefined with respect to any process. The love simply is! The Aorist tense most commonly expresses His love as a simple fact without reference to any process (BUR, p.19). We have been loved just as Jesus has been loved. His love is a fact! Count on it!

God, the Father, loves me like He loves Jesus. Mind boggling! How can we explain a truth like this?! We are so identified with Jesus that we are loved infinitely in Jesus. *"I in them and you (the Father) in me,"* Jesus prayed. The depth of our union with Jesus expresses the depth of the Father's love for His Son.

Our unity shows God's love to this world.

John 17:24-26

Father,
24 Πάτερ,
    Whom you have given to me
    ὃ δέδωκάς μοι,
I will
θέλω
    that
    ἵνα
        where I, myself, am
        ὅπου εἰμὶ ἐγὼ
        in addition they might be with me,
        κἀκεῖνοι ὦσιν μετ' ἐμοῦ,
            in order that
            ἵνα
                they might see my glory,
                θεωρῶσιν τὴν δόξαν τὴν ἐμήν,
                    which you have given to me
                    ἣν δέδωκάς μοι
                        because you loved me
                        ὅτι ἠγάπησάς με
                            before the foundation of the world.
                            πρὸ καταβολῆς κόσμου.

Righteous Father,
25 πάτερ δίκαιε,
    The world indeed has not known you,
    καὶ ὁ κόσμος σε οὐκ ἔγνω,
but I have known you,
ἐγὼ δέ σε ἔγνων,
    and these ones have known
    καὶ οὗτοι ἔγνωσαν
        that you, yourself, sent me,
        ὅτι σύ με ἀπέστειλας·
and I have made known to them your name
26 καὶ ἐγνώρισα αὐτοῖς τὸ ὄνομά σου
And I will continue to make (it) known
καὶ γνωρίσω,
    in order that the love (with) which you loved me
    ἵνα ἡ ἀγάπη ἣν ἠγάπησάς με
        might be in them
        ἐν αὐτοῖς ᾖ
        and I in them.
        κἀγὼ ἐν αὐτοῖς.

JOHN 17

PREACHING POINTS

The repetition of the vocative, "Father," provides the clue to the two main preaching points in this segment. The two preaching points revolve around the will of Jesus and the revelation of Jesus. Jesus explains His purpose in each of these expressions. The purpose behind each expression relates directly to our lives today.

Central Idea:

1. (v. 24)

2. (vs. 25-26)

Briefly, identify two contemporary life parallels to these verses.

CLP #1

CLP #2

HIS LAST WILL

Jesus wills us with His last, irresistible will to be with Him in His glory (John 17:24). *"Father, whom you have given to me, I will that where I am they may be with me in order that they continually see my glory which you have given to me because you loved me before the foundation of the world."* He wills us to join Him in Heaven because true lovers long to be together forever!

Jesus' will is more than a want or a desire and far more than a wish. Jesus no longer asks the Father. He expresses His will for us to the Father which, taken in the context of impending death, is more like His last will and testament (GDT, p. 903). *"I will"* (θέλω) is a "quasi-imperative" (HAN, p. 180). He wills that we be with (μετ') Him. The preposition suggests being in close association with another person (BAGD, p. 508).

The verb θέλω, when used of God in the Old Testament, refers, all but once, to the sovereign will of God, resolute and unbending. The resurrection power of the Son in perfect harmony with the Father gives life to whomever He wills (θέλω, John 5:21). Jesus' will determines whether John lives or dies before the return of Christ (John 21:22). It is a matter of His will (TDNT, 3:47-48).

Jesus wills that we be with Him to continually see (θεωρῶσιν) His glory. The present tense verb indicates an ongoing seeing, not a one-time seeing. The verb carries the sense of being a spectator or observer of His glory (BAGD, p.360). We will see His glory continuously when we are with Him forever.

Here is not the glory Jesus had before the world began (John 17:5). Here is the glory the Father gives to the Son after He completes His saving work on earth. Jesus' pre-incarnate glory is nowhere said to be given to Him. His pre-incarnate glory is His by who He is as eternal God (MEY, pp. 472-473). Jesus speaks here of His glorious reward proleptically as if it has been given (δέδωκάς) to Him already, so certain is He of the completion of His work. He wills us to see His glory, a glory certain yet not yet seen.

We will be with Him because He wills us to be with Him!

PERFECT LOVE'S PRESENCE

The purpose of Christ's revelation of God to us is the presence of His perfect love in us. Jesus closes His priestly prayer for us with these words dripping with tears of love. *"I have made Your name known to them, and I will make it known, so that the love with which You loved Me may be in them, and I in them"* (John 17:26).

The Father's love for His only Son is the same love that lives in us. God revealed Himself to us in His Son for the express purpose of making His love live in us. The expression *"the love with which you loved Me"* (ἡ ἀγάπη ἣν ἠγάπησάς με) is called a "cognate accusative" (BD, p. 85). It is a Semitic idiom consistent with the Hebrew style of writing that John often displays. The noun (ἀγάπη) is followed by the same root as an Aorist verb (ἠγάπησάς) to form a cognate accusative (MHT, 3:245).

The cognate accusative expresses the content of the Father's love (ATR, p. 477). The inner content of the Father's love for us is His love for the Son. He loves us with the same love He possesses for His only Son. It is not merely - if we can ever use such a word to describe God's love - the fact that He loves us. Jesus prays that God's love might be "in them" (ἐν αὐτοῖς) so, by extension in us.

God's perfect love lives in us. It is not just that God loves us. God intends the inward presence of His perfect love to fill our lives. God's purpose is that His perfect love will rule our lives and govern our relationships (MEY, p. 475). We can love others with God's love because God's love is present in our hearts in a way that was impossible for us as unbelievers. Perfect love is in us because Christ is in us! His presence creates the capacity for our love which is why Jesus adds "and I in them" (κἀγὼ ἐν αὐτοῖς).

There is a rich and precious implication of these words that we should not miss. The Father loves the Son who lives in us! God's love does not attach itself eternally to sin, so the object of perfect love is the perfect Christ living in us and reproducing His life in us (GDT, p. 905). Nothing can separate us from the love of God in Christ (Romans 8:39) because Christ is in us, and nothing can separate the Son from the Father (John 17:26).

Love is the perfect end to His priestly prayer for us because love is the end of God's eternal purpose for us.

"But now faith, hope, love, abide these three; but the greatest of these is love" (1 Cor. 13:13).